APPLIQUÉ

A PRACTICAL APPROACH
TO DESIGN AND CONSTRUCTION

ISBN 0 7134 5349 4

Typeset by Servis Filmsetting Ltd, Manchester
and printed in Great Britain by
Anchor Press, Tiptree, Essex
for the publishers
B.T. Batsford Ltd
4 Fitzhardinge Street
London W1H 0AH

APPLIQUÉ

A PRACTICAL APPROACH

DOROTHY TUCKER

B.T. BATSFORD LTD
LONDON

ACKNOWLEDGEMENT

I would like to thank: my husband Terry Rollinson, for coming to the rescue with a word-processor, and for all his support; my father, for typing and editing my hand-written scripts, and my mother, for her sustaining interest and eye for detail; my family and friends, for their forbearance and encouragement when times seemed hard; the Practical Study Group, students at the Blackheath School of Art and Roehampton, and many other embroiderers who generously shared their ideas and have allowed their work to be included. Particular thanks to Bill Robertson for photographing so many items, to Herta Puls for her help with the section on molas, and to Constance Howard for her generous and invaluable support over the years.

CONTENTS

INTRODUCTION

How many people realize that when they stitch a patch over a hole in a pair of trousers or an old jacket they are carrying out a form of appliqué? From this simple idea springs a whole range of practical and decorative sewing techniques, which combine both traditional and modern elements of the craft.

The word appliqué comes from the French verb 'to put on'. In some notes published by the Victoria & Albert Museum, London, it is defined as 'the sewing of patches to the surface of a material so they form a pattern either by their own shape and colour, or by the shape and colour of the ground material'. Both of these definitions hint at the enormous variety of applications and definitions contained in the simple word appliqué.

Look around you and you will readily see how many garments, fabrics and household items make use of appliqué. Linen, lingerie, children's clothes, window blinds and cushions are just a few notable examples. By looking in churches and museums you will also come accross a whole range of other, more traditional forms of the craft, particularly on quilts and ecclesiastical embroideries.

Today, contemporary textile and embroidery exhibitions have also challenged and extended the concept of appliqué. Look closely for ways in which design and fabric, stitch and construction depend on each other and you will begin to discover the extent to which appliqué can be as much about construction as decoration; it is about making new textiles from small pieces of material as well as creating pictures and patterns. With both the traditional and modern applications in mind, I have compiled many exciting ideas for you to try and delight in.

Besides showing you how to carry out different methods, with particular emphasis on design and construction, I have also included advice on which material to use with which technique. The projects and design sheets will provide you with simple starting points to give you the know-how and the confidence to carry out your own pieces. The extension ideas at the end of each section are also there to encourage you to explore further, with ideas for combining techniques and creating alternative textiles.

Remember that achieving a satisfactory piece of work is sometimes more demanding than you might expect and often requires several attempts before you succeed in making what you intended. I have chosen many pieces because they illustrate the best of their kind rather than the easiest. It took time, practice and experience to create them. I hope that in discovering how they were made you will appreciate them and their making with increasing insight and enjoyment.

1 *Detail of a fish skin coat, Eastern Siberia, nineteenth century.* (Victoria & Albert Museum, London)

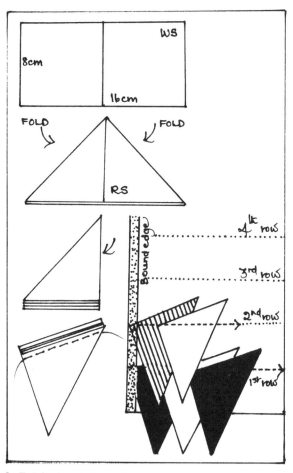

2 *Folded patchwork.*

3 *Points of folded fabric, 15 × 26cm (6 × 10in),
Asta Ḱristinsdottir, 1987.*

1 FOLDING, CUTTING AND APPLYING

FOLDING AND APPLYING

One of the most direct ways of designing for appliqué is to cut into a folded piece of fabric, open it out, and then place this cut-out shape onto another piece of fabric. Yet even before you pick up your scissors, it is interesting to explore the number of different ways in which you can apply folded pieces. Small scraps of patterned dark and light coloured cottons folded and applied together can create beautiful colour combinations and kaleidoscopic effects. Simple ideas lead to unexpectedly stunning or subtle designs: for example a strip of colour interrupted with a series of coloured triangles, lines of alternating dark and light points, pattern or colour variations repeated in squares, blocks and circles. These can be built up into bold and simple forms or very complex ones and provide inspiration for details and finishing touches. Other materials, such as leather, felt, paper and plastics can be combined with fabrics to create faceted surfaces and constructions.

The Lisu hilltribes of Thailand make a delicate form of appliqué by folding very fine cottons into triangles and sewing them between narrow colourful strips to form the sleeves and yokes of their blouses. In a similar way, you can make a chunky form of folded patchwork by folding rectangles of cloth into points and applying them in overlapping lines of alternating dark and light colours to create bold patterns. Many variations of mitred patchwork are based on squares or rectangles of fabric folded into right-angled triangles. The first four triangles are often arranged to form a central square from which all the others radiate.

Adding gathers to folded material is also effective. A square of fabric folded into a triangle and then gathered along the lower edge will form a petal shape. A circular patch folded into half and gathered along the curved edge will form another petal variation with neat little pleats. The Victorians made mats of these by applying them around the outside edge of a circle and then in decreasingly smaller, overlapping rings until they reached the centre. In Brazil and Turkey all sorts of rugs are made from fragments of folded fabrics, and Indian textiles provide a rich source of ideas for details and finishing touches for quilts, clothing and wall hangings.

FOLDED POINTS AND BLOCKS OF PATTERN
(fig. 2)

This chunky form of folded patchwork is made by applying points of folded fabrics in lines onto a foundation cloth:

☆ Cut rectangles, approximately 8 × 16cm (3⅛ × 6¼in) from strips of coloured cottons and fold each three times to form points.

☆ Apply the first line of points down along a guide line drawn above the lower hem of a background cloth; set each point at an angle to overlap with its neighbour and to jut out beyond the hem.

☆ Secure these by a line of machine stitching or running stitch.

☆ Arrange a second row directly above the first, the points angled to cover the raw edges and stitching of the previous row.

☆ Build patterns with each new row by running a series of points in different colours.

4 *Detail of wrong side of strips with folded points from Thailand.*

5 *Details of strips with folded points, 14 × 26cm (5 × 10in). (Courtesy of Vicky Lugg)*

☆ Finally, neaten the raw edges around the top and sides of the whole piece within a band of matching cotton.

The effect is essentially bold and bulky.

STRIPS AND POINTS
(fig. 6)

For lines of small folded triangles the Lisu hill-tribes of Thailand use fine, closely-woven cottons in plain bright colours torn or cut with the straight grain into narrow strips. Some strips become the bands and others make the triangles. The Lisu use very narrow strips, but for practice it may be easier to begin with strips about 2.5cm (1in) wide. The width of the strips, however, will depend on the weight of the fabric and the purpose of the appliqué.

☆ Take a strip of fabric and press under a 6mm ($\frac{1}{4}$in) turning along its length. Make a rectangular template of the required size and mark and cut the rectangles. Fold each rectangle into a triangular point by bringing the shorter pair of sides together to the centre.

☆ To make the bands, sew a strip of cotton onto a similar strip with a running stitch, right sides and edges together and then turn it down. This leaves a slight ridge. Several more strips in different colours can be added in this way.

☆ Tack the points in place on the last strip, the open end of each slotting neatly around the folded side of the next. Cover this line of points by the next strip and stitch into place from the wrong side with a running stitch. Then turn the strip back to expose the triangular points and so on.

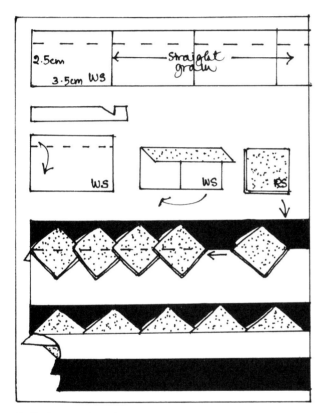

6 *Strips and points.*

EXTENSION IDEAS

Because this kind of appliqué is made from a series of narrow strips joined together without a foundation fabric, it can be stitched to stretch and curve slightly, particularly if the strips are cut on the bias. Extend the technique by including fabrics with tiny prints or silks. You could also place the triangles differently, or perhaps apply them in different sizes or in double pairs. On a larger scale single triangles of leather, plastic or other non-fraying fabrics could be applied between strips.

TRIANGLES FROM SQUARES *(fig. 7)*

Some variations of mitred patchwork are based on small squares of fabric folded into right-angled triangles and applied in overlapping lines. Folded squares are particularly appropriate for thin or transparent fabrics, materials which fray easily and articles which are going to be washed frequently.

☆ To make a mitred triangle, cut a square measuring 5 × 5cm (2 × 2in) from a strip of fabric. First fold the square in half and then fold the top corners to the centre base and press flat.

☆ Starting from the top edge and building downards place the triangles in horizontal rows onto a matching foundation fabric and secure each triangle with four small stitches worked over the corners.

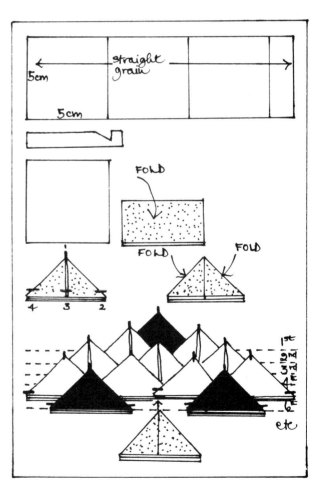

7 *Triangles from squares.*

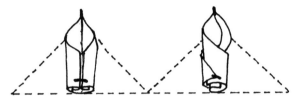

8 *Rolled triangles.*

9 *Pockets of partially applied squares of muslin with gold lamé, surrounded by strips of Madras cotton and a border of mitred patches. 16 × 16cm (6 × 6in), Dorothy Tucker, 1977.*

FOLDED STARS *(fig. 10)*

Folded star or mitred patchwork is made from small patches of contrasting fabrics, folded into right-angled triangles, applied onto a foundation fabric. The central fold lines of these patches give the work its mitred character. Although the arrangement of mitred triangles varies, it frequently forms star designs.

Closely woven, summerdress-weight printed cottons or poplins, lawns and ginghams are suitable to use on a foundation of pre-shrunk sheeting or calico. A mix of polyester and cotton makes fabric springy and more resistant to creasing; it may need extra pressing. Good quality sewing thread should be matched to the colours of the patches.

☆ Select several different prints and colours. Cut the fabrics into 3cm ($1\frac{1}{4}$in) strips with the straight grain. Press a 6mm ($\frac{1}{4}$in) turning to the wrong side along one long edge. Then along each strip mark and cut out 5cm (2in) rectangles.

☆ To make the triangles fold the top corners of the rectangle (or folded square) to the centre of its base and crease flat.

☆ In the centre of a foundation fabric, mark a 5cm (2in) square. Through the centre of the square draw a vertical and a horizontal line and then the diagonals, extending them all beyond the square. With a broken line mark the bisecting lines between these by drawing a circle and dividing each section into half with a compass.

☆ Stretch the foundation fabric into a ring or onto a frame.

☆ *1st row:* Select four triangles. Pin the first triangle with its folded edges in line with the vertical and horizontal lines and secure its point to the centre with a tiny stitch. Apply the other three triangles to complete the square and secure them with a stitch across the corners of each triangle 5mm ($\frac{1}{5}$in) within the outside edge.

☆ *2nd row:* Select eight triangles to contrast with the first four. Stitch each of them about 12mm ($\frac{1}{2}$in) from the centre of the square; four triangles to overlap the first row with mitres diagonally in line, then the other four with mitres in line with the vertical and horizontal lines. The patches should lie as flat as a hand of cards.

☆ *3rd row:* Select 16 triangles. Place and stitch the point of each triangle equidistant from the centre of the square with their points on the lines of the 16 divisions, overlapping each other in a circle.

☆ Finally, trim the outside edge and bind or neaten within a matching facing.

10 *Folded stars.*

CIRCLES OR TRIANGLES (fig. 11)

This variation of mitred patchwork is based on concentric circles of applied, right-angled triangles with the points facing away from the centre to form a neatened outer edge. The raw ends of the innermost row of triangles and the remaining space are covered with a decorative centre, perhaps a circle of cloth or a rosette of ribbons and lace, beads or a covered button, raised embroidery stitches, knots or loops, padded circles, squares or other applied shapes.

☆ Make a card template of a circle with a radius of 6.5cm (2½in) and divide it into 16 divisions. Stretch the foundation fabric in a ring or over a frame. Tack around the template to transfer the circle to the fabric and mark the 16 points. Tack across the circle making 16 divisions.

☆ Select at least three or four contrasting fabrics. Cut the fabrics into 3cm (1¼in) strips with the straight grain. Press a 5mm (¼in) turning to the wrong side along one long edge. Then along each strip mark out and cut 5cm (2in) rectangles to form mitred triangles.

☆ 1st and 2nd row: Around the circle place eight triangles pointing outwards in line with alternate markings. Apply with a stitch across each corner and through the point. Then apply another eight between them to complete the circle.

☆ 3rd row: Apply eight triangles with their points 1cm (⅜in) from the points of the first set of triangles (1st row).

☆ 4th row: Apply another set of eight between these with their points 2cm (¾in) from the points of the circle.

☆ 5th row: Apply eight triangles with their points 3cm (1¼in) from the points of the first circle.

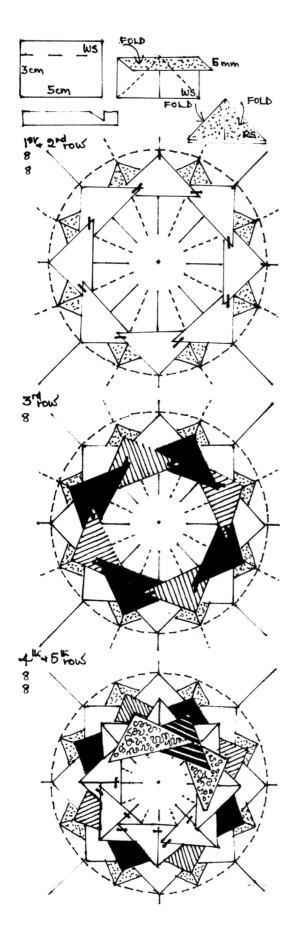

☆ *6th row:* Apply a final row of eight triangles 4cm (1½in) from the points of the first circle, overlapping one another. Trim off the corners and cover the raw edges in the centre by applying a cloth square or circle. Alternatively, to make a feature of the overlapping corners cut a separate set of rectangles, allowing for extra turning. Turn in both raw edges before folding to make a neatened triangle.

PETAL PATCHES
(fig. 12)
Petal shapes can be made of fine fabrics such as gauzy synthetics, silk organzas, organdie and lawns.

☆ Fold a square patch of fabric diagonally in half and diagonally again to form a folded triangle.

☆ Sew a line of running stitch through all four thicknesses along the lower edge of the triangle. Then draw the thread up. The gathers will form a petal shape (fig. 12c).

Another petal shape can be made by folding a circle of fabric in half. Sew a line of running stitch through the curved edge and then draw it up. This usually gathers up into neat pleats at the petals' base (fig. 12c).

Petal patches are usually applied from an outer edge inwards, each row overlapping the previous one and decreasing in number towards the centre. Neaten the raw edges of the final row by applying a circle of cloth or a covered button.

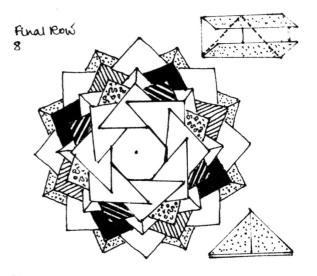

11 *Circles of triangles.*

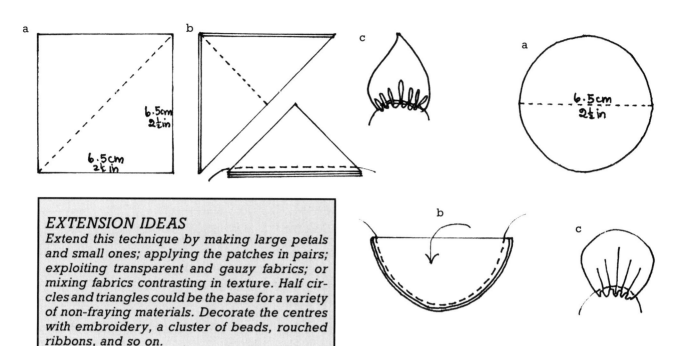

12 *Petal patches.*

FOLDING AND CUTTING

The technique of folding and cutting is used in various ways in northern India. Many of the applied shapes characteristic of Rajasthani appliqué are made simply by folding fabric and cutting into the folded layers. Opened out, these cut-out shapes are laid in patterns on fabrics of a contrasting colour (colour plate 5 and fig. 13). The edges of the patches are turned under and sewn down with blind hemming, running stitch or back stitch. In the Kutch region different communities assert strong tribal indentities through their clothes, which are richly embroidered. Embroidery is valued for its

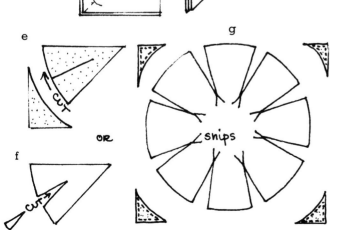

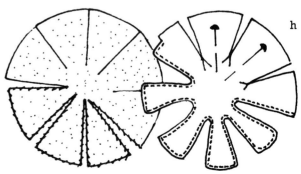

13 *Flowers from folded circles.*

14 *Square from a Rajasthani quilt.*

beauty and commercial value; a family's wealth and status is recognized by the quality and number of quilts, household covers and bags in its homes. Cut scraps of fabric are applied onto new or used backgrounds, which may have been re-dyed or pieced together or both. Often women will transform worn clothing into pieced and applied textiles of great beauty.

SAW-TOOTH POINTS
(fig. 16)

☆ Cut a strip of fabric 5cm (2in) wide with the straight grain, allowing 1cm (⅜in) for a turning. Measure and mark equal sections along its length, either by folding and creasing or by measuring.

☆ Tack the strip into position onto a fabric in a different colour. Cut down alternate folds in turn to approximately 1cm (⅜in) above the lower edge.

☆ Fold the cut edges back to form a row of triangles and stitch along the saw-tooth points with running stitch or invisible hemming (fig. 16).

On some Rajasthani appliqués these saw-tooth points are neatened or enhanced with crosses of interlaced herringbone stitch (colour plate 6).

☆ Cut a strip of fine cotton with the straight grain to measure 10 × 72cm (4 × 32in). Fold it in half along the length. Fold backwards and forwards into four sections (fig. 17a,b,c)

☆ Press flat, then fold top left and right hand corners to centre base. Press flat. Cut out shapes from the diagonal folds (fig. 17d,e).

☆ Unfold and open out.

☆ Place the strip of cut patterns onto a contrasting fabric. Turning under all the cut edges, apply the strips with tiny backstitch.

On the pillow cover (fig. 20) notice the way in which the very small cuts are made into larger shapes.

☆ *Cut a square of fine cotton 21 × 21cm (8 × 8in). Fold it diagonally in half and press flat. Fold the triangle in half and press flat.*

☆ *Cut out shapes from the folded sides.*

☆ *Open the square out. Place it onto a contrasting fabric.*

☆ *Turning under all the cut edges apply the patch 'with tiny backstitch (fig. 17g).'*

On the pillow cover (colour plate 6) notice the silk pompoms and pearls and the lines of interlaced herringbone embroidered in the spaces.

15 *Detail from an appliqué quilt from Rajasthan, 45 × 45cm (18 × 18in).*

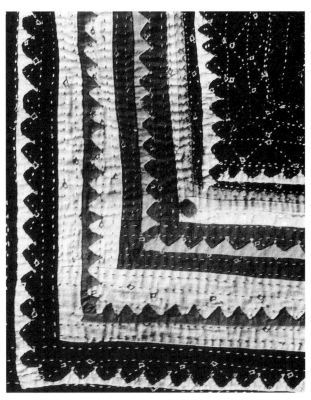

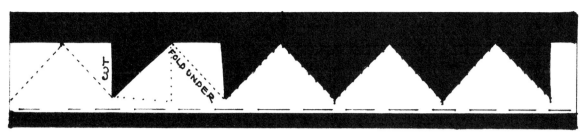

16 *Saw-tooth points.*

17 *Saw-tooth cuts.*

a

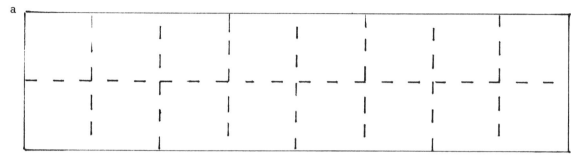

b

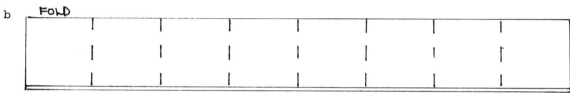

c 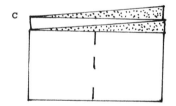   d   e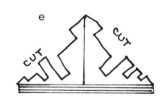

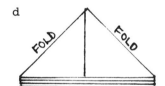

f

g

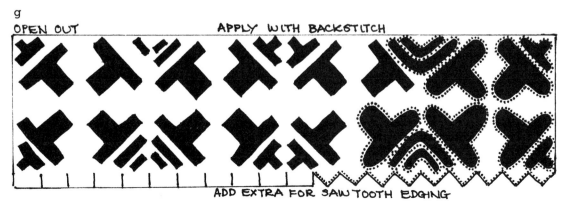

EXTENSION IDEAS
Linked chains of figures or animals cut from
strips of folded fabrics can be applied around
the hems of clothing. Try out an idea from
design sheet 1 (appendix).

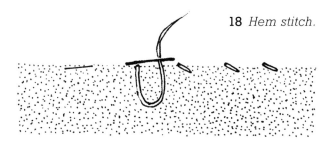

18 *Hem stitch.*

19 *Scalloped cuts.*

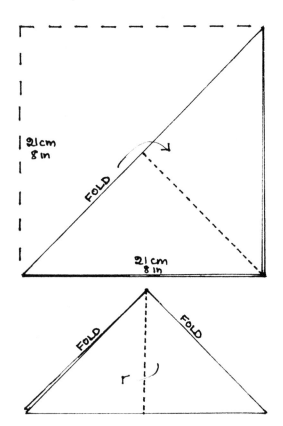

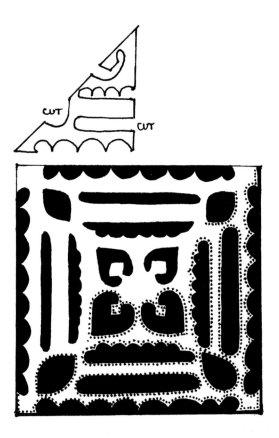

20 *Detail of the pillow case in colour section.*

BACKSTITCH (fig. 21)

Backstitch is often used for outlining. It is worked from right to left. Make a straight stitch to the right and bring the needle out a stitch length further along. Then take a backward stitch to the end of the first one again, bringing the needle out two stitch lengths further along. Take another backward stitch and repeat.

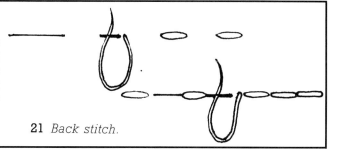

21 Back stitch.

HERRINGBONE (figs 22, 23 and 24)

Herringbone is often used to apply shapes with cut edges or fabrics which fray. Rows or blocks of herringbone stitches are effective for decorative borders and form the basis for interlaced lines and crosses. Without picking up any fabric, the row of herringbone stitches can be laced with matching or contrasting thread using a tapestry needle. For tiered rows the stitches must be very evenly spaced.

Working from left to right, bring the needle out on the lower line. Moving to the right, take a small stitch on the upper line from right to left with the thread below the needle. Again, moving to the right, take a small stitch on the lower line from right to left with the thread above the needle and so on.

Thread: *coton à broder No. 6; flower threads; coton perlé No. 6.*

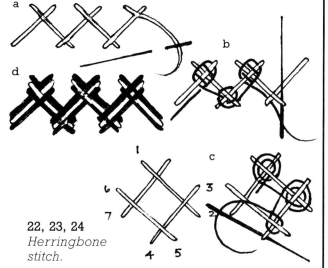

22, 23, 24 Herringbone stitch.

Needles: *betweens or sharps size 7; tapestry needles for lacing.*

SHISHA WORK (fig. 25)

Shisha work originates from northern India and Pakistan and is made by stitching small pieces of mirror glass or mica onto fabric.

Hold glass with left thumb, bring needle out at lower left (1). Take thread across glass, put needle in on right and bring out directly above (2). Then, take the thread across to the left and bring needle out at the bottom (3). Pass needle under first thread, pull through and pass under thread above (4). Put needle into fabric (5) and bring out to the right (6). Then pass needle under threads as before (7). Fasten securely on the back with a little stitch. Bring the needle out again below the glass on the far left (8). Pass needle under first intersection and bring out to the right of working thread (9). Make a small stitch alongside glass with thread under the needle (10). Pass needle under vertical thread, bring out with thread under the needle (11). Make another stitch up alongside the glass with thread under the needle (12) and so on right around the glass.

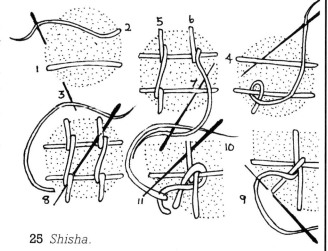

25 Shisha.

Thread: *flower threads; coton perlé No. 6; coton à broder No. 6; floss silks.*

Needles: *betweens size 7; a tapestry needle for lacing.*

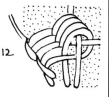

PROJECT 1
A SQUARE FOR A CUSHION, A BLOCK FOR A QUILT

You will need:
- *thin paper*
- *pencil*
- *coloured paper*
- *ruler*
- *sharp, pointed scissors*
- *tape measure*
- *pins*
- *betweens or sharps needle size 7*
- *tacking thread and fine strong sewing thread*
- *coloured pieces of medium weight closely woven cotton e.g. percale or broadcloth*

1 Select three fabrics ranging in colour from dark to light. Decide which is to be the background. Measure and cut this into a 50cm (20in) square. Crease this in half and half again to establish the centre. Choose the fabric for the central patch and cut a 20cm (8in) square from it.

2 Fold several 20cm (8in) squares of thin paper into quarter triangles (fig. 19). Cut into the folds to create different patterns. Alternatively, cut out design A or B from design sheet 2. Use it as a template. Simply place it on a folded square and trace and cut out the pattern.

3 Open out all the paper patterns and choose one of them.

4 Now fold the central patch into quarter triangles and, using the paper pattern chosen, cut out the shapes. Unfold, open out and place the patch centrally on the background fabric, straight grain with straight grain. Secure it with a grid of tacked lines, run about 5cm (2in) apart across the design. Starting from the centre and working outwards, turn under the cut edges and sew with backstitch, snipping now and again to ease curves and corners. Notice how, on the Rajasthani pillow cover, some cut-out spaces have been joined up where the fabric was too narrow to turn under.

5 Finally, cut the the remaining fabric into small, complementary patterns by using smaller designs placed on smaller folded strips and squares. Arrange these around the central patch in an attractive way.

EXTENSION IDEAS
This simple design idea could be imaginatively extended to include pompons, lines of herringbone or shisha work, saw-tooth points, rows of mitred patches, or applied triangles. You could use it to make a cushion or a square within a quilt where different variations in colour or pattern are pieced together in interesting ways.

26 *Twentieth-century Hawaiian quilt, 211 × 191 cm (83 × 75in). (The American Museum in Britain, Bath)*

All Hawaiian motifs are symbolic. The symbols recur in different combinations. This pattern represents Queen Kapiolani's fan and Kahilis cut from red cotton applied to a white cotton background.

27 *Contour quilting.*

Running stitch is traditionally used for quilting. The stitches should be very even but not too dominant. Depending on the thickness of the quilt, the stitch length varies between 3–6mm ($\frac{1}{8}$–$\frac{1}{4}$in). The lining, wadding and top fabric are tacked together and quilted through all three layers, the lines of stitching closely following the irregular contours of the applied design.

28 *Cut appliqué from Thailand, 16 × 16cm (6 × 6in). (Courtesy of Vicky Lugg)*

Curved and linear designs are drawn onto the folded top fabric and partly cut through with a series of interrupted snips, then tacked onto the background fabric. The cut edges are turned under with the needle and neatly hemmed. The bridges of cloth between the snips that have kept the design intact are cut on the way.

CUT APPLIQUÉ

American cottons reached Hawaii in the early nineteenth century. The ladies of the royal household were the first to quilt and children were taught to sew in mission schools. Hawaiians love to combine two brilliantly contrasting colours, perhaps red and green, or to set a strong plain colour on a white background.

Hawaiian quilt designs are cut from a single piece (design sheet 3). The four- or eight-rayed balance of positive and negative shapes is so effective that it is sometimes difficult to decide which is the applied piece and which the background. The designs, often inspired by leaves and fruit, are cut to open out into one large complex piece, (design sheet 3). The four- or eight-rayed shape, a basic fold-and-cut pattern, provides a strong design structure for the intricate outlines and the lines of quilting closely contouring them. The padding is very thick. Traditionally, each quilt is given a special name, such as the Comb of Kaiuland or Garden Island.

29 *Cut appliqué from Thailand, 60 × 60cm (24 × 24in). (Courtesy of Cecilia Barclay)*

30 White Wall, *78 × 51cm (30 × 20in), Vicky Lugg, 1984.*

A huge, single cut shape sets up a continuity within the design which is quite different from simple cut-out repeats or the folded and cut strips and squares which pattern typical Rajasthani covers. On a much smaller scale, another form of cut appliqué which has this quality comes from the Blue Meo and White Meo hilltribes of north west Thailand. But there is a significant difference. Their patterns are created by folding and snipping a series of curved and straight cuts into the top fabric of a contrasting pair of pieces of exactly the same size. The raw edges of these cuts are turned under and hemmed so that channels of the background piece of fabric appear to form patterns in a series of repeats that follow the geometry of the fold lines and contrasting colour.

In Thailand, embroidery is valued so highly that a legend tells of a Yeo woman creating the earth by sewing the land together and pulling up the mountains with a needle. The Yeo tribe wear trousers embroidered all over with a particular kind of crosstitch worked into handwoven cloth. The White Meo and Blue Meo hilltribes wear skirts made with six yards of indigo-dyed cotton, hand painted with batik patterns and finely pleated. Bordered heavily with embroidery these sway

alluring from the hips, although the focus of the White Meo costumes is on the appliqué belts and collars which flap back to display eye-twisting geometrics and curved linear designs worked on the underside. A woman's prestige depends on her sewing skills, and the inventiveness of her designs is intended to attract the beloved. New clothes are made for the New Year festival – always a very important occasion, particularly for unmarried girls.

Many people from these tribes have become refugees. Various aid projects, supported by the Thai royal family, enable some of them to earn an income from their traditional skills. Fabric and threads are now imported, and increasingly cloth is cut and colours combined for items designed for the western market.

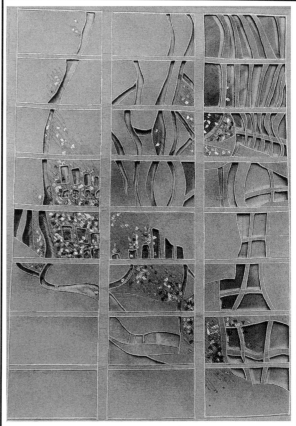

31 Reflections, *100 × 66cm (39 × 26in), Moyra McNeill, 1983.*

Reflections is based on shapes seen in a glass-fronted tower block in Croydon. The panel is poplin bonded onto pelmet Vilene (Pellon) with areas of the design cut away. The satin stitch machining round the shapes used 1,300 metres 1,420 yards) of thread. Parts of the design are spray-painted with applied fragments of lurex fabric, trapped onto the surface by machine stitching.

32 Tulips, *18 × 16cm (7 × 6½in), Solvig Starborg.*

This line drawing is made from one of Solvig's many photographs of tulips (fig. 32). She simplified it and blocked in the background spaces to adapt it for a design for cutwork (fig. 33). She then traced this drawing onto thin card to make a template around which she drew to transfer the design onto a piece of fine white cotton.

Using stranded embroidery cotton, she covered the outlines in closely worked buttonhole stitch with the looped edge to the outside of the flowers and leaves. When the sewing was complete she cut away the background shapes with very sharp, pointed scissors close to the stitching. Finally, she placed the cut panel onto a softly padded background of silk and bound the edges to make a bag with a quilted strap (Fig. 34).

33 *Revised drawing of the tulips. First they were traced on card, then cut out to make a template and stencil to transfer the design onto the fabric.*

In some work, lines of running stitch divide the channels. Blocks and dots of embroidery are worked on large uncut areas to keep the layers of fabric together. Although usually invisibly hemmed, a large stitch and a little extra tension in sewing creates an indented edge. Some cushion covers worked in this way have a beautifully textured surface after they have been washed.

CUTWORK

Although cutwork and appliqué seem to be directly opposed techniques, they are, in fact, closely related. A shape cut out from a piece of material leaves an equivalent space. This 'negative shape' can provide an equally satisfying design. In appliqué the notion of negative space – the relation between positive and negative shape – is all important.

Many beautiful and complex forms of textile decoration, such as broderie anglaise, renaissance work and richelieu, have evolved from the idea of cut-out spacing forming the design. In more elaborate forms of cutwork the cut-away areas are bridged with decorative bars or 'brides' and embellished with 'picots'. In reticella, for example, large cut-away areas are filled with intricate needlelace patterns. In traditional work self-coloured thread is used and the outlines of cutwork are usually embroidered in the buttonhole stitch. It is essential to use very closely woven fabric and to avoid fabrics that fray.

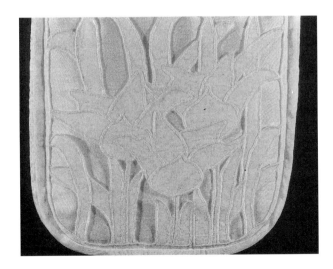

34 *Cutwork bag, Solvig Starborg.*

PICOTS

1 Once the outlines have been covered with buttonhole stitch, the looped edge facing the areas to be cut away, bars or foundation threads for needle weaving can be made by passing the working thread across from outline to outline, bridging the shapes without picking up the fabric. When bars are complete carefully cut away the areas beneath them to leave lacey spaces.

2 To make picots work buttonhole stitch to the centre of the bar, insert a pin into the bar and background fabric at right angles to the bar. Loop working thread under the pin then up over the bar and out underneath. Slip needle under the loop and over the bar. With thread under needle continue with buttonhole stitch. Remove pin, pull loop tight.

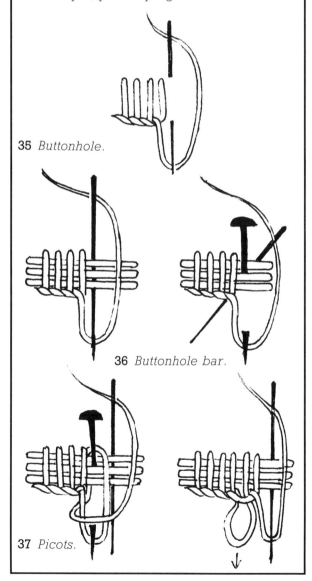

35 *Buttonhole.*

36 *Buttonhole bar.*

37 *Picots.*

PROJECT 2
CUTWORK BUTTERFLY

You will need:
- drawing paper, thin white paper, black paper, tissue paper
- pencil
- paper scissors
- glue
- water-soluble transfer pen
- sharp, pointed embroidery scissors
- sharps and betweens needle size 7
- very closely woven cotton
- matching sewing thread

1 Make a simple line drawing of the butterfly on design sheet 4.

2 Trace and cut out the design on white paper. Place on black paper to see areas which are to be cut away clearly. Revise where necessary, then glue down.

3 Transfer the design onto fabric directly with a transfer pen or by first tracing the design onto tissue and then stitching through the tissue and the fabric, following the outlines, with running stitch. Then tear away the tissue.

4 Add another line of running stitch parallel with the first.

5 Over the foundation of these two rows of stitching, work closely spaced buttonhole stitch with the looped edge facing the areas to be cut away.

6 Then, as close to the stitching as possible, carefully cut out the spaces within the stitching.

EXTENSION IDEAS
Extend this idea by either adding embroidered details or more butterflies or repeating the design, perhaps overlapping some. Picots or needle weaving could be incorporated. A larger design could be machined with satin stitch – this is quicker to work, just as strong and also reversible, opening up the possibility of using transparent fabrics. Coloured threads could be used provided that they do not override the positive and negative quality of the design.

Transparent effects

Many transparent fabrics such as organdie, silk organza, fine silks and lawns, nets or sheer synthetics lend themselves to cutwork and appliqué techniques. Designs for lingerie often combine two or three different transparent fabrics applied together with various areas cut away, and the play of light on fabric surfaces is often attractively exploited by cutting designs from the dull reverse side of a fabric, such as satin and applying them onto the shiny side.

On a larger scale some linens, hung against a window, will let the sunlight through beautifully.

Simple outline drawings, for example the tulip design by Solvig Starborg (fig. 32), can be traced onto tissue paper or lay-out paper. A light-box may be helpful in planning a cutwork design.

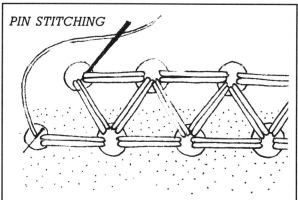

39 *Pin stitching.*

Three-sided or pin stitching is an effective way of sewing applied shapes on fine fabrics because it is very flat and strong. As well as being reversible and travelling around straight and curved outlines both decoratively and easily, it is also a useful joining stitch, particularly for the seams of undergarments made of delicate fabrics.

For practice, pin stitching could be worked around the outline of the tulip from design sheet 6. Trace and transfer this onto two fabrics placed together.

Closely stitched herringbone could be used for the narrow stem, worked on either the right side, or from the wrong side to give a shadow effect.

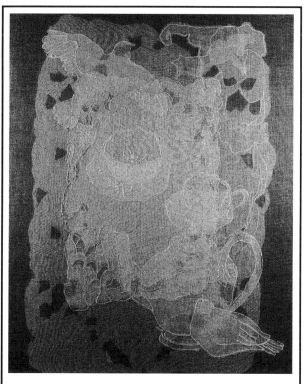

38 Afternoon Tea, *70 × 50cm (28 × 20in), Pamela Hamilton, 1985.* (Courtesy of L. Haurahan)

Pamela Hamilton likes to base her work on familiar, everyday things around her but feels she only knows them intimately when she sits down and draws them. She like to create a sense of thoughtfulness or a mood. She works by simplifying her drawings and superimposing them on each other often combining unrelated objects. She traces her designs onto organdie and machines through several layers, often using the free stitching foot, and then cuts away the unwanted areas.

☆ Place two fabrics together and the traced drawing on top. Transfer the design by tacking through the tracing and the fabrics. Then slit the paper under each tack with a needle and gently lift away the tracing paper.

☆ Now with a single thread and a size 4 crewel needle, pin stitch through both layers following the outline.

☆ Finally, cut away one layer of fabric close to the stitching.

A more open effect can be created by pin stitching using a larger needle and a finer thread. A zig-zag effect can be created by pulling more tightly on the thread. Stiffening the fabric with spray or liquid starch may help to give a firm surface to work on with the advantage that afterwards the starch washes out completely (see page 58).

EXTENSION IDEAS

These techniques could be tried out by adapting the butterfly on design sheet 4 or the rose on design sheet 5. The idea could be extended by reducing or enlarging the design on a photocopier and then spreading several copies together over a light-box. A very fine machine satin stitch could be used instead of the pin stitching.

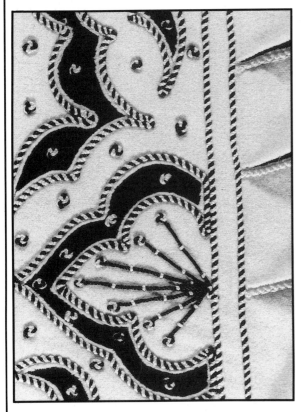

40 *Detail of a late nineteenth-century French collar, made from fine cream wool cut out and applied onto black wool. Notice the whipped couched cord neatening the outline and the decorative couching and knots. (Courtesy of Constance Howard)*

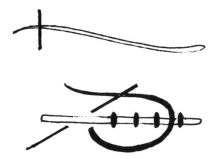

41 *Couching.*

COUCHING

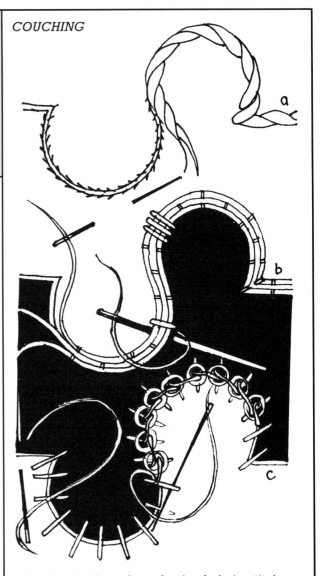

42 *Couched cords and raised chain stitch.*

Twisted cords can be couched invisibly by using a matching thread and inserting the needle between the loosened strands (a). Couching with a contrasting colour can be decoratively arranged in simple patterns (b). Embroidery stitches, e.g. variations of raised stem band or raised chain band worked on a laid foundation of threads provide other effective ways of securing and masking the joins (c).

The colour, tone and width of these can appear to increase the area of a shape. A thick outline in red will tend to extend a red shape and encroach on a neighbouring area so care must be taken not to upset the balance of a design by overloading the outlines.

43 The Cavendish Hanging, *late sixteenth century.* (Victoria & Albert Museum, London)

The Cavendish Hanging is one of the Oxburgh hangings. It is made of green velvet decorated with the monograms and emblems of Mary Queen of Scots and Bess of Hardwick. These have been embroidered with silk in cross stitch onto linen canvas and then applied. The cut edges of the 'badges' are covered with a padded band of gold satin stitch flanked by couched cords. The joins in the velvet cloth are masked by formal coiling flower patterns, couched to fill the spaces lightly and link the shapes.

SLIPS

In the thirteenth and fourteenth centuries velvets were covered with a very fine linen and the embroidery worked through the two layers plus a linen backing. When the stitching was complete, the surplus areas of linen were cut away and the cut edges neatened with cords and couching. The church embroidery of this period, 'Opus Anglicanum', is rich with examples of this.

The embroidered motifs and sprigs that powdered the surfaces of English embroidery in the fifteenth and sixteenth centuries were worked separately on fine linen in coloured silks and metal threads. These were then cut out and applied to velvets and other precious fabrics. The edges were covered with couched threads or braids or sometimes padded satin stitch. Scroll patterns were often couched directly onto the velvet in the spaces between the applied 'slips'. This was a device which helped to mask any joins in the cloth and linked the applied motifs together.

Another way of applying patches worked on linen is to cut round the work wide of the outline and fray back the linen. Then thread up each frayed end in turn and use it to apply the shape.

VELVET

Velvet is a beautiful fabric but it is difficult to apply because of its pile, which is easily crushed and marked. Christine Risley, in her book *Machine Embroidery** includes a method for applying velvet in which, instead of stretching velvet in a ring, the design is stamped onto a stiff linen. This is placed face down with the background fabric and then the velvet placed on top, right side uppermost. All three fabrics are turned over and two lines of running stitch following the design marked on the linen are worked down through the background fabric and the velvet. The velvet is then turned right side up. The surplus fabric is trimmed away and the edges then corded. The linen may finally be cut and frayed away too.

*Christine Risley; *Machine Embroidery – a complete guide.* Studio Vista, London, 1973, page 19.

CUT AND INTERCHANGE

When shapes cut from a fabric of one colour are applied to a second coloured fabric and the remaining shape from the first fabric is in turn applied to the second, positive/negative patterns are formed (fig. 46a).

In counter-change designs the light shapes on dark grounds alternate with their opposites as dark patterns on light grounds in a perfectly balanced exchange of positives and negatives. Colour and pattern can be interchanged quite simply in this way or in more complex series (fig 46b).

INLAY

Inlaid work differs from appliqué but, like cut-work, is a closely allied technique. Applied designs are cut and stitched **onto** a background. Inlay involves setting patterns **into** cut surfaces. In its most classical form, both the design and its background are cut from different fabrics to fit together on a foundation fabric like a jigsaw puzzle, the positive and negative shapes perfectly interlocking. To achieve this the fabrics are often placed together and the design cut through both layers. The shape from one layer then fits into the other exactly (fig. 46c).

The interlocking shapes are hemmed into place with the cut edges perfectly flat and butted together to cover the foundation fabric beneath them. The raw joins are then strengthened and neatened by perhaps cords, couched, twisted hanks of thread or braids.

The bold, formal outlines of inlaid work and its constructional strength make it perfect for banners and flags, copes and chasubles. Many interesting examples are to be found in church embroidery.

When the cut edges of inlaid areas are turned under and hemmed, a channel of the background fabric is exposed between them. This provides a third colour in the design. Many examples of this can be found on Indian appliqué and mola blouses (figs 46d and 47).

45 *Raised satin.*

44 *Padded satin.*

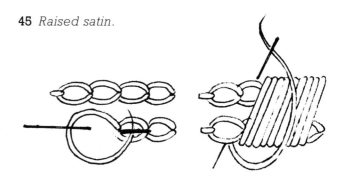

46 *Inlay.*

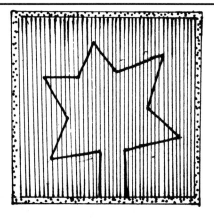

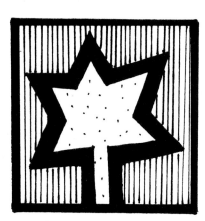

47 *Inlay.*

PROJECT 3
INLAY JIGSAW

You will need:
- *fabric for a foundation square, e.g., calico*
- *two fabrics to inlay which contrast in colour, pattern or texture*
- *matching sewing thread, tacking thread*
- *complementary cords, braids or threads to couch*
- *a rectangular frame*
- *pins and needles (sharps No. 7 and crewel No. 10 for couching)*
- *water-soluble marking pen, chalk pencil, etc.*
- *paper scissors*
- *pattern drafting paper (optional)*

All fabrics should be washed and ironed flat, and cut and applied with the straight grain.

1 Stretch a foundation fabric 40 × 40cm (15¾ × 15¾in) over the frame.

2 Mark out a grid for nine 8.5cm (3¼in) squares. Add a 2.5cm (1in) border all round.

*3 Either: mark a similar grid onto the wrong side of both inlay fabrics and draw in the design using the quarter template cut from design sheet 7. Then cut out the shapes.
Or: draw the design out on patterned drafting paper, marking out the grid first and filling shapes with the three quarter template from design sheet 7. Place paper pattern securely onto fabrics, either singly or together and cut out the shapes.*

4 Pin the jigsaw shapes in place, alternating the fabrics, with the cut edges butted together. (The remaining pieces make a second panel.)

5 To secure the shapes, hem over the cut edges around the outlines with a matching thread with widely spaced overcasting.

6 To neaten the joins, select and couch over with cords or braids or threads, such as, soft embroidery cotton, perlé cordonnet, tapestry wools or gold metal threads. These could be couched singly, in several rows or grouped together. Textured yarns can also be interesting.

EXTENSION IDEAS

Try breaking up the jigsaw design or encroaching on areas with couching. You could piece the design together to make a picture. Alternatively, the chequer board pattern could include many different fabrics or areas of embroidery. The foundation fabric need not be completely covered; some pieces could be missing or in disorder.

PROJECT 4
CUT, FOLD AND INTERCHANGE

You will need:
- *fine smooth cotton fabric in three contrasting colours*
- *a fine pencil or transfer pen or tailor's chalk*
- *a very sharp scalpel and cutting board or very sharp, fine-pointed embroidery scissors*
- *needles and pins*
- *tacking thread and sewing threads to match fabrics*

1 Cut 15 × 18cm (16 × 7in) rectangles from each of the fabrics with the straight grain. Select one as the background layer. Cut the design out from design sheet 8 to make a card template (or plan a design of your own remembering that a shape on a fold doubles its width and the shapes must link up).

2 Place two layers of fabric together both with right sides uppermost and fold them lengthwise into half and fold them again widthwise into quarters.

3 Place the template on the folded cloth so that shapes will link, after cutting, across the folds. Trace round the design. With sharp scissors, from an open edge of the folded quarter, cut through all the layers along the design line.

4 Unfold and separate the two layers. Sort out the cut shapes interchanging the colours to make two sets of contrasting pairs. Arrange each set on a background fabric so that the colours and designs interlock, their cut edges butting up to one another. Tack down the centre of each band to keep the shapes in place.

5 Then, starting from the centres of the designs, turn under and hem all the cut edges, snipping carefully into corners where necessary. As the sewing is completed the background fabric will be exposed, giving a third channel of colour.

6 Remove the tacking.

EXTENSION IDEAS

The design can be extended by folding a proportionally larger rectangle into eight, even sixteen areas, depending on the weight of the fabric, or by piecing several sections of the design together. The bands within the design could be made twice the width and carry a narrower version of the same design applied on top, so creating a five-layered or five-coloured appliqué. You could leave some of the 'floating' shapes out, substitute them with embroidery, or replace them with a completely new colour for an asymmetrical effect.

SUGGESTED READING
Paul and Elaine Lewis. *Peoples of the Golden Triangle.* Thames and Hudson, 1984.
Patricia Lambert, Barbara Straepelaere and Mary Fry. *Color and Fibre.* Schiffer.

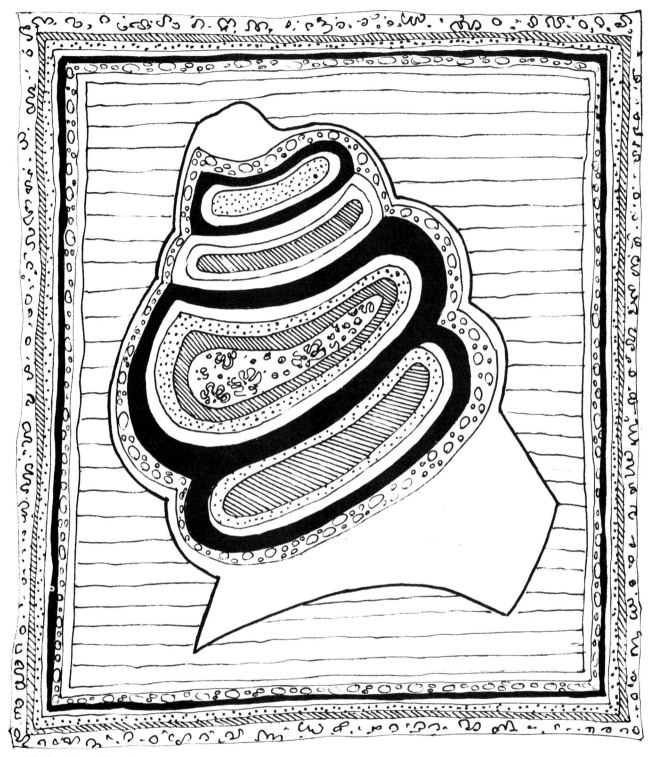

48 *Shell appliqué.*

This is a drawing of layered appliqué based on a shell made by Elizabeth Beasley. It is worked through eight layers of printed and plain cotton polyester. She found it was possible to make a series of templates from one design by cutting away the sections just completed and drawing the next around them. Starting from the

top layer, she cut out the largest areas and hemmed the outside shapes to a layer added underneath. On the final layer only a very small kidney shape was stitched surrounded by unattached fabric. The piece is bulky, very stretchy and weak when pulled, but this can be remedied by stitching through all the layers afterwards in an interesting way.

2 MULTI-LAYERED APPLIQUÉ

In multi-layered appliqué the design is assembled by progressively applying one layer after another onto a background fabric or by cutting back layers of fabric to expose the layers beneath. Simply stitching four or five layers of fabric one on top of the other, even if some layers are later cut away, produces a very bulky, rigid textile. Amanda Smith's *Meat Pieces* is an interesting example of this (see colour plate 7). She has used cut work and a layered appliqué technique to translate her studies of meat carcasses into textile form. Up to 20 layers of fabric ranging from calico to deep red are stacked and machined together, then cut to expose raw edges of colour and so sculpt the disturbingly beautiful shapes and forms.

When in 1963 McCall's *Needlework and Crafts*, a national magazine produced in the United States, reproduced pictures of three mola blouse panels made by the Kuna Indians, very few people had ever seen one first hand. In an attempt to describe how they were made, the term 'reverse appliqué' was coined. Although the term is an over simplification of the mola making process and misleading, 'reverse appliqué' was taken up as a new idea and enthusiastically developed.

EXTENSION IDEAS
Layered appliqué need not be limited to designs based on outlines within outlines or the use of cotton fabrics. Muslins, gauzy synthetics, silks, fine leathers and felt, even plastics and paper can be combined together. Simple grids can be machined onto several fabrics stacked together then cut or slashed to expose layers of different colours and textures. Areas can be cut and slashed from the front and back of the work. This idea could be explored using the grid on design sheet 9. Trace the design and transfer it onto the top fabric in the stack or make a template of a unit and draw it into a grid tacked
through all the layers. It could provide a way of creating interlaced patterns of Celtic crosses and strap work, mazes and knot gardens.

Layered appliqué can be combined successfully with other forms of appliqué and effectively linked with other sewing techniques. It can be used to frame other pieces of work. The contours of indented ridges created through layered appliqué and cutwork techniques have interesting design links with the carved surfaces of relief sculpture and other three-dimensional work.

49 *A grid machined onto layers of dyed cotton winceyette and muslins with squares of fabric cut away to expose different levels. 27.5 × 21.5cm (11 × 8½in), Dorothy Tucker.*

PROJECT 5
LAYERED APPLIQUÉ

You will need:
- *gauzy and transparent fabrics, e.g., nets, synthetic chiffons, or silk organzas in several different colours. Or coloured muslins, lawns or fine cottons*
- *a fabric transfer pen, tailor's chalk or pencil*
- *greaseproof paper*
- *a sewing machine*
- *matching sewing thread*
- *sharp, pointed embroidery scissors*

1 Draw a simple grid or network of shapes or use the grid on design sheet 9. This will repeat and could be photocopied and enlarged.

2 Measure the design and cut the fabrics with straight grain into matching rectangles or squares.

3 Decide on the sequence of colour. Lay one fabric on top of another.

4 Set the machine to straight stitch – a fairly short stitch length makes it easier to turn on curves and corners. Test how many layers of cloth together will feed through the machine readily and adjust the stitch length and tension to cope with them.

5 Transfer the design onto the top fabric. Place this back on the stack, and run a line of tacking stitches around the outside edge of the pieces to keep the layers securely together.

6 Machine along the design lines starting from the shapes in the centre and fastening off ends on the way. Finally, surround the panel with a line of machining to enclose all the shapes.

7 When the machining is complete, layers of fabric from the front or back of the piece can be cut away to expose layers below, leaving the cut edges contouring the spaces. Remember, enough fabric must remain to keep the piece intact.

EXTENSION IDEA
Studies of cellular structures are a marvellous source for networks of interesting shapes.

MOLAS

KUNA ART AND BELIEF

Mola making is a complex, multi-layered process that combines a variety of appliqué, cutwork techniques. Mola is the Kuna word for cloth, but is used to mean either the front or the back panel of a blouse. The Kuna live on a strip of land and over three hundred tiny islands known as the Cormarca de San Blas along the Caribbean coast of Panama where they maintain a highly independent lifestyle. Until the 1960s very few people knew about the Kuna and their molas, but now with the development of tourism, their work is sought after.

Molas seem to have evolved from borders of cut and applied designs which eventually broadened into a pair of panels and combined up to six colours. The designs include birds, animals and plants as well as geometric and symbolic patterns. Fine multi-coloured lines of chain and running stitch are often used to add more detail.

Women work most of the designs and since the Kuna are thrifty they save and use every scrap of fabric. The remaining pieces cut from shapes applied on the front panel are frequently sewn into the design on the back panel, but a motif is never repeated in exactly the same way. Innovation is much admired by the Kuna, and new ideas are spurred on by a sense of competition. It is their ingenious balance of technique and colour and a wealth of designs which make molas a unique art form.

A stylized lizard is still drawn in black lines down a girl's nose to protect her from harm. Many mola designs are similar to the old picture writing and symbolic patterns associated with tattoos and the tribal body painting practised in the seventeenth century. The Indians themselves can no longer explain many of the old symbols. They believe that every human, animal and plant has a soul and that after death the soul travels through the fourth layer of an eight layered underworld where the chiefs and evil spirits reside. Herta Puls, in her book *The Art of Cut-Work and Appliqué*, wonders to what extent this idea is symbolically expressed in the multi-layered process of mola making.

Although printed fabrics were used in older molas for a complete layer, in later ones patterned fabrics are sometimes sandwiched between the layers. Traditionally, fine trade cottons are used in solid, vivid colours.

(Right:) **50** *Mola panel, 32 × 45cm (13 × 17½in).* (Courtesy of Constance Howard)

51 *Mola panel 39 × 47cm (15½ × 18½in). (*Courtesy of Constance Howard)

52 *Detail of mola panel (colour section), 47 × 52cm (18½ × 21½in). (*Courtesy of Constance Howard)

53 *Detail of stitching on back of mola panel, fig. 52.*

THE KUNA'S USE OF COLOUR

The Kuna are very aware of the balance between colour and shape. In a well designed mola the appliqué and the background shapes are equally balanced and interesting.

Colour is an essential dimension to mola design, with red, black and orange predominating. Primary colours – reds, blues, and yellows – and the secondary colours – orange, green and purple – are often juxtaposed to create shifting planes and optical illusions. Visually, the colours function independently from the actual layers of cloth. With the right intensity a colour, such as green, ringed with its complementary, red, will appear to 'sizzle' because each colour produces an after image of the other. In many linear designs pairs of complementary colours alternate with the lines in which only one of the colours is found by itself, or is teamed up with another colour, for example, lines of red surrounded by turquoise. This produces multiple visual sizzle. In a three-colour mola the eye first pairs with the alternating lines of applied colour and then with just one of the applied colours and the background. It is this visual see-saw which makes areas of colour seem to shift. The background, depending on its colour, can make everything else seem to float in front of it. In a four-coloured mola the background disappears, the less intense colours drop back and the bright come forwards. The channels of black, often the exposed background layer, separate areas of strong colour in much the same way as veins of lead in stained glass windows. The black prevents the colours from affecting one another and merging together and so keeps them vibrant and intense.

It is difficult, without handling a mola, to appreciate fully its flatness, flexibility and strength or to see exactly how appliqué and cutwork can be combined in several layers of cloth. As the mola is built up from the base, layer by layer, all the work is completed in each layer before the next is added and the design depends upon the decisions made in a previous layer. In each layer more shapes can be applied onto any part or a layer cut to show the colour beneath it (colour plates 3 and 4). The cuts can be whole shapes or narrow slits, or small triangles and circles, often called 'nips and pips' (figs 54 and 55). The combination of cutwork appliqué and embroidery ensures that the background and foreground shapes are broken up so that no large area of colour remains. Patches of additional colour are sometimes sandwiched between one layer and the next, or a whole layer is made up of different coloured strips laid next to each other (fig. 55).

One of the ways to understand how a mola design is constructed is to work out the order in which the layers have been stitched. Each layer is a different colour, but it is not as simple as this. The order appears to change because, while some parts of a layer are simply left out within each layer, other areas are cut and interchanged with colours from another layer to form interlocking designs, and more colours are applied on top. It is this interchange of shapes within each layer which gives the molas their flatness. The colours in each layer are cut to fit into the spaces between the shapes already applied. This is a complex and unique form of inlay. As the cut edges of the inlayed shapes are turned under and hemmed, a channel of the fabric to which they have been applied is exposed between the shapes to give a third colour (see figs. 46d and 47).

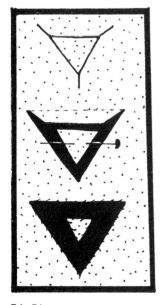

54 *Pips.*

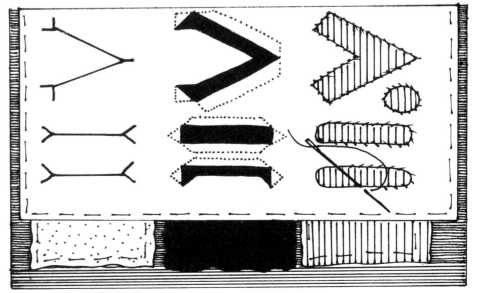

55 *Slits.*

Mola designs are marked out with pencil lines or cut directly into the cloth. Another way is to cut through two layers together with a series of small interrupted snips which keep the shape intact. The layers are then separated and the cut designs interchanged, one after the other. The Kuna know what they want to achieve and build up a design layer by layer. They cut either following lines of tacking or the stitched edge of the previous shapes which they can feel through the fabric to be applied next.

All the cut edges are turned under and neatly hemmed right through all the layers in matching thread. This gives a slightly quilted appearance and also gives the work its strength. On the wrong side is a tracery of stitches in which the different coloured threads outline all the pieces applied. This is a typical and particularly beautiful feature of molas (figs 52 and 53).

Embroidery stitched in a contrasting colour can give a design extra impact as well as keeping larger areas of embroidered cloth together. The stitching can sometimes appear to change the colour of an area. The multi-coloured lines and spirals of chain or running stitch are often very elaborate on modern molas – a blouse can take up to two years to complete. From beginning as a substitute for the time-consuming cutwork and appliqué involved in some of the finest examples, embroidery on some molas has developed into a special feature in its own right.

PROJECT 6
MOLA MAKING

You will need:
- fine smooth closely woven cotton in three different colours
- scraps of fabrics in other colours
- greaseproof paper and pencil
- sharp, pointed embroidery scissors
- needles and pins
- tacking thread in two colours
- sewing thread to match fabrics

1 Choose a design from design sheet 10 and trace this onto tissue paper.

2 Cut 18cm (7in) squares out of three different fabrics.

3 Decide which fabric is to be the background and lay one of the other two on top with the straight grains matching.

4 Pin the tracing on top of these. Run a line of tacking around the outline through both fabrics, marking corners clearly and keeping the fabrics as flat as possible (a).

5 Remove the tracing by slitting through the paper underneath each tack on the surface of the work with a needle and lift off the paper carefully, leaving the tacks behind.

6 To prevent the layers from separating, run a line of tacking in a different colour around the outside edge of the design (b).

7 Cut through the top layer of fabric within the outline allowing enough margin for turnings (b). (The shape cut free can be saved and applied onto another panel (fig. 57).)

8 Snip through the tacks which mark the design and carefully lift the fabric away so that the tacks remain in the layer below.

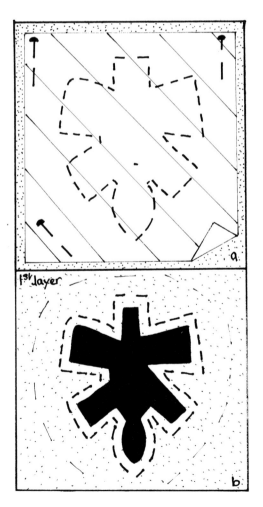

56 Method for making mola.

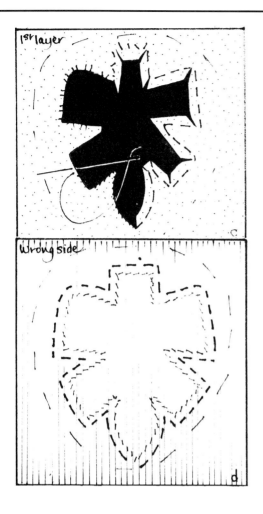

15 The second shape cut free can be applied onto a second panel with the first piece cut free applied in turn on top of it (fig. 57).

16 Snip through the tacks and carefully lift the fabric away so that the tacks remain in the layer below.

17 Now turn under the cut edges of the second layer towards the outside of the design so that the folded edge lies on the line of cut tacks and the first layer and background colour is exposed.

18 Snip where necessary to ease a corner or curve (f).

19 Then sew through all three layers with invisible hem stitching in matching thread (f).

20 Shapes of different colours could be inlaid into the space on the first panel. The applied shape in the second panel could be patterned with small cuts which, turned under, expose the layer beneath.

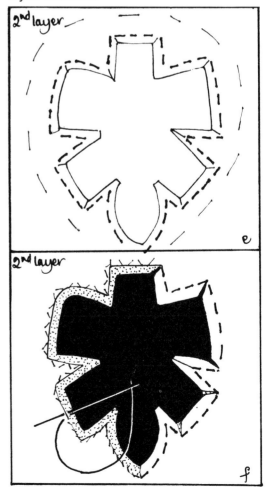

9 Now turn under the cut edges of the first layer towards the outside of the design, so that the folded edge lies on the line of cut tacks below and the background colour is exposed. Snip where necessary to ease a corner or curve (c).

10 Then sew through both layers with invisible hem stitching in matching thread (c).

11 Place the next square with straight grain matching on top of the first applied layer. Run a line of tacking around the outside edge of the square in a different colour to hold the layers together.

12 Turn the work over to the wrong side. Mark the second outline 0.5cm (¼in) outside the first with another line of tacking (d).

13 Turn the work back to the right side.

14 Cut through the second layer of fabric within the tacked outline allowing enough margin for turnings (e).

57 *Shape applied to another panel.*

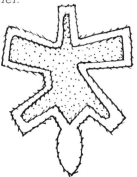

EXTENSION IDEAS

Having mastered this method, you could make a more complex design by combining several motifs. Explore various design ideas by making card templates and drawing around them onto coloured papers. Different arrangements could be made with the paper cut-outs. Cut the same shape out several times to make repeats or turn it over to give a mirror image. These will suggest sequences of work and will show you where sets of shapes could be interchanged and inlaid, or areas could be cut in various ways to expose the layers beneath them, or where more shapes could be applied.

Remember a paper design may need to be cut and spaced out in places in order to allow enough space between the fabric shapes for turnings.

Finally, try working very fine lines of running or chain stitch to give extra details and keep the layers together.

PROJECT 7
AN INLAID MOLA PATTERN

You will need:
- fine smooth closely woven cotton in three different colours
- fine hard pencil, transfer pen or tailor's chalk
- very sharp scalpel and cutting board
- sharp, pointed embroidery scissors
- needles, pins and tacking thread
- sewing thread to match the fabrics

1 Select one fabric for the background and cut two 18cm (7in) squares for a front and back panel.

2 Cut an 18cm (7in) square from each of the other two fabrics.

3 Place these two together, right sides up and with the straight grains matching.

4 Either: transfer the line drawing from design sheet 11 onto the top square. Or: draw two continuous parallel lines which are never less than 2.5cm (1in) apart from each other.

5 On either side of this line, at least 1cm away, make a series of interrupted snips with scissors or cuts with a scalpel through both layers.

6 Then separate the two squares.

7 Place each cut square on a background square and tack it securely in place midway between the snips.

58 *An inlaid mola pattern.*

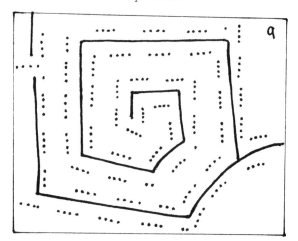

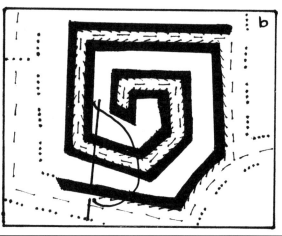

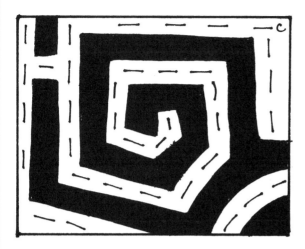

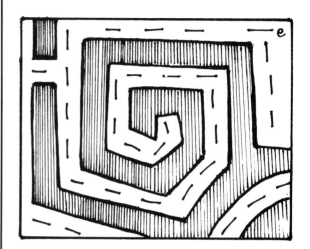

8 On each panel, starting from the centre, turn the cut edges under towards the tacked line and hem, snipping through the bridges just ahead of the stitching.

9 As the cutting and sewing is completed a shape of fabric will be cut free. Save this.

10 To complete the design, when the first layer on both panels has been stitched, interchange the 'negative shapes' cut free from each square. Lay them in turn between the patterns just applied. They should fit perfectly.

11 Tack them in place midway between the cut edges. Turn under and hem as before.

12 The channel of background fabric exposed between the two inlaid colours provides the third colour in a design. In mola designs inlaid patterns like these can be used to fill the spaces between picture shapes.

EXTENSION IDEAS

These two panels need not be lined. Several different ones could be pieced together in interesting ways. The pair of panels could be joined to make a bag. They could be incorporated into log cabin patchwork and become the feature of a cushion or garment. They could be enhanced and extended by strips of saw-tooth edging. They could be laced over card to form the sides of a box.

SUGGESTED READING

Anna Parker and Avon Neal. *Molas – Folk Art of the Cuna Indians*. Baire Publishing, Clarkson N Potter Inc., Crown Publishers Inc., 1 Park Avenue, New York 10016, 1977.
Mari Lyn Salvador. *Yei Dailege! Kuna Women's Art*. The Maxwell Museum of Anthropology, The University of New Mexico, Albuquerque, New Mexico, 1978.
Charlotte Patera. *Mola Making*. New Century Publishers Inc., 1984.
Herta Puls. *The Art of Cutwork and Appliqué – Historic, Modern, and Kuna Indian*. B.T. Batsford Ltd., London, 1978.
Rhoda L. Auld. *Molas. What they are. How to make them. Ideas they suggest for Creative Appliqué*. Van Nostrand Reinhold Company, 1977.

59 *Garden wreath quilt, 221 × 180cm (87 × 71 in), nineteenth century. (The American Museum in Britain, Bath)*

In this quilt, alternate patchwork and appliqué blocks are surrounded by a border based on a variation of the wandering tulip pattern. The tulip was introduced into Europe from the east in the middle of the sixteenth century. Its simple shape and strong colour appealed particularly to settlers in America from Germany and eastern Europe and is to be found in many Pennsylvanian quilts.

3 PICTURES AND PRINT

PATCHWORK

Patchwork and appliqué quilts were equally popular in America between the late eighteenth and nineteenth centuries. The early American quilts were made from scraps of good cloth saved from worn clothing and randomly pieced together. In time, the cloth was cut and joined to make simple 'hit or miss' brick patterns and the idea of building designs by different arrangments of triangles and squares evolved. Whereas patchwork construction in Europe was based on the repetition of a single geometric unit, usually a hexagon or diamond, in America quilts were pieced together in lap-size blocks. The blocks were easier to hold and sew, and practical to store. Each block was completed separately and then several were joined together to link up across a whole spread and form a larger overall geometric design. Favourite blocks were known by special names, such as, Jacob's Ladder, Clay's Choice, Road to Oklahoma, and Storm at Sea (fig. 60). These were passed on and used again and again in different combinations, and new ones were invented.

Whereas patchwork involves piecing together hundreds of small pieces of fabric side by side, appliqué involves sewing small patches onto larger ones. But the techniques are often combined. A number of blocks such as basket, triple sunflower and triangle flower are made from both pieced patches and appliqué. First, the regular geometric shapes are pieced together to form the block and then the curved and irregular parts are applied afterwards (figs. 60, 61 and 62).

Hearts, vases of flowers, birds, berries, and leaves were favourite patchwork-appliqué motifs. Traditionally, these shapes were cut out of spot and sprig cotton prints in greens, pinks and reds, sometimes with plain yellows or blues. The shapes

60 *Block of patchwork appliqué.*

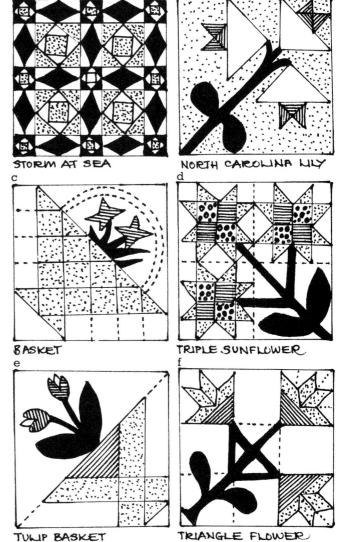

a
STORM AT SEA

b
NORTH CAROLINA LILY

c
BASKET

d
TRIPLE SUNFLOWER

e
TULIP BASKET

f
TRIANGLE FLOWER

61 *Patchwork and appliqué.*

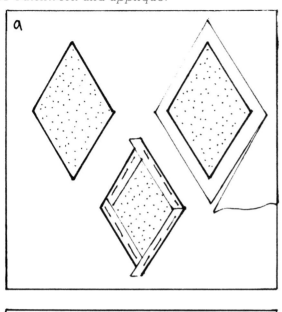

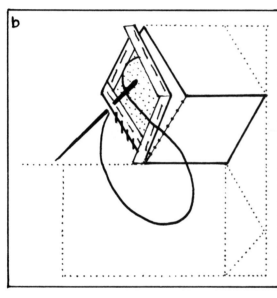

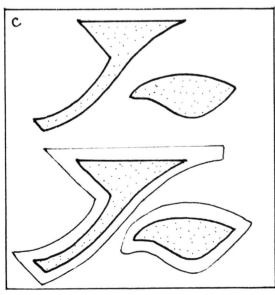

62 *Quilting.*

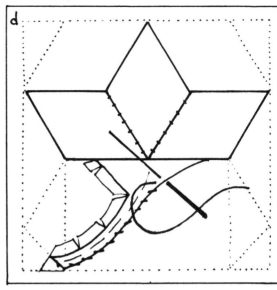

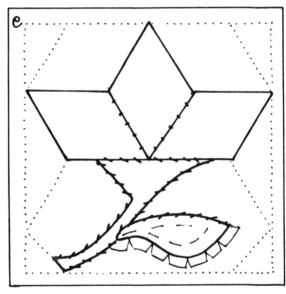

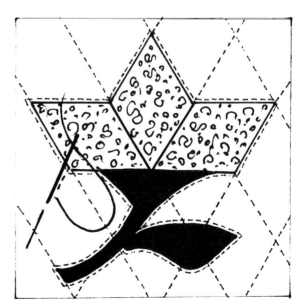

63 The Baltimore Bride Quilt *(colour section),*
*314 × 314cm (122 × 122in), 1847. (*The American
Museum in Britain, Bath)

Some of the best album quilts were made in the
Baltimore area between 1846 and 1852 by a
group of young women, amongst them Achsak
Godwin Wilkins and Mary Evans, who met
through the Methodist Church and worked
together to make quilts for their friends and for
the benefit of the Church.

Brides' quilts always include hearts. On this
quilt, they can be seen at the ends of the bands of
patchwork used to piece the appliqué blocks
together.

It is well worth going to the American
Museum in Britain to look at the quilt at first
hand. Although some of the blocks were made
from professionally drawn patterns, the quilt is
a dictionary of patchwork appliqué techniques
and invention.

Parts of large printed patterns have been cut
out so that the colours suggest shading on some
shapes (5). It includes numerous examples in
which small pieces of fabric have been sand-
wiched between the appliqué and background
fabric and the applied shape cut to give patterns

1	2	3	4	5
6	7	8	9	10
11	12	13	14	15
16	17	18	19	20
21	22	23	24	25

on a vase or veins on a leaf (13,7,15), or perhaps
pips in a fruit (25) or to suggest opening buds in
the border of flowers. The Kuna Indians have
developed this idea in a quite unique way to
make their mola blouses (see fig. 52) In some
parts petals have been padded with loose
cotton stuffed under the applied shapes (17) or
several layers of petals have been applied one
on top of the other to give a slightly raised effect
(6). Elsewhere flower centres are filled with
simple cut spirals similar to the cut and applied
patterns of mola designs (24) and basket effects
created by a lattice of overlaid strips (7,17).

were sewn with tiny invisible hem stitching onto squares of white or unbleached cotton (fig. 61). The motifs were arranged in wheels, circles and garlands set within a grid of squares, mirroring patchwork construction – the garden wreath quilt illustrates this very well (fig. 59). They were also assembled in blocks with the repeats following the design lines of a folded square, both across and diagonally, again like patchwork. Sometimes a quilt was a checkerboard of different blocks particularly if it had been made by a number of women working together, as they often did for wedding and friendship quilts. *The Baltimore Bride* is a particularly fine example of this (fig. 63). Presentation quilts made to commemorate a special occasion, perhaps for a local church, often recorded events in picture form and included the town's buildings and characters.

Whereas joining pieces together side by side tends towards a rather graphic geometric construction, appliqué is free form and open to being more expressive and personal. Although many appliqué quilt motifs have names, such as Rose of Sharon, and were borrowed and adapted from professionally drawn patterns or bought in kit form, others were original and beautifully drawn and cut out. Each bird or leaf is seen in a single shape, a silhouette of colour against a ground of white and set in a kind of space achieved through colour contrast with neighbouring shapes. Stencil like, these rarely overlap. Their simplicity of line, form and colour places them with the best of American decorative folk art.

EXTENSION IDEAS
The quilts from the American Museum are classic and rather formal, but the twin techniques of patchwork and appliqué could be used to create geometric structures of colour, overlaid with free-form shapes. Images come to mind of plants against walls and amongst flagstones, or the fragmented lettering and images of tattered posters on street hoardings. Drawings and photographs of these would provide some interesting design ideas.

PATTERNS ON QUILTS
On American quilts the pattern on a vase or the veins in a leaf is sometimes made by inserting pieces of fabric under an applied shape which is slit and stitched back to show the contrasting piece sandwiched between it and the background. This is a simple version of inlay. The Kuna Indians have developed this form in a combination with cutwork and appliqué in a unique way to make their mola blouses (figs 64 and 65).

PROJECT 8
FLOWERS AND FRUIT

You will need:
- *a selection of plain and printed cottons in reds, yellows and blues*
- *a square of unbleached, pre-washed cotton, 50 × 50cm (20 × 20in)*
- *a square of thin cotton wadding 50 × 50cm (20 × 20in)*
- *a square of backing fabric 50 × 50cm (20 × 20in)*
- *matching sewing threads and tacking thread*
- *a fine needle and sharp scissors*

For patchwork appliqué use fabrics which are firm, non-stretch and pre-washed to prevent shrinking. Fabrics of different kinds and strengths, e.g., old and new, should not be mixed and very worn cloth discarded. Use fine cotton or sewing silk in as fine a needle as possible so that the stitching is not too obvious.

1 Make a template from design sheets 12 or 13.

2 Place this on the wrong side of a coloured or printed fabric and draw around it with a pencil line, yarn needle or tailor's chalk on dark fabrics. (Pencil lines tend to mark the thread and can leave dirty patches which are difficult to wash out.)

3 Cut out the shape, allowing extra fabric for turnings (use a template to cut out several shapes).

4 Place this on the square of unbleached cotton and tack well within the cut edge.

5 Apply with tiny hem stitching, snipping into the curves and corners where necessary.

6 Before an outline is completely stitched, either sandwich scraps of fabrics in a contrasting colour between the applied shape and the background, cut the top layer, turn under and hem to give extra patterns (figs 64 and 65). Or: push small amounts of stuffing between the layers to give a raised effect (fig. 119). Or: apply more shapes on top.

7 By using different templates from design sheets 12 and 13 and cutting out fabric shapes from various prints and colours, compose a vase of flowers or bowl of fruit. You can also repeat shapes in decorative bands around a circle or to form a square.

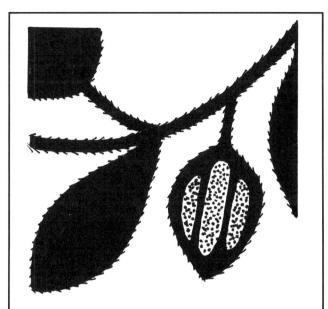

64 and 65 *Inlaid patches.*

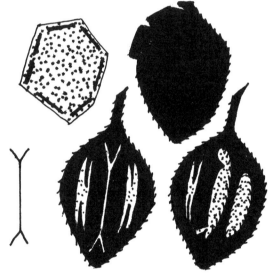

8 *Finally, place the piece on a thin layer of wadding and a backing fabric. Secure all three layers together with a grid of tacks and quilt with parallel lines of tiny running stitches to run diagonally both ways across the remaining background space. Sometimes a line of quilting is worked close to the outline of the applied shapes to give a nice finish and a slightly raised effect.*

EXTENSION IDEAS
Add embroidery to supply fine details. Piece together or surround appliquéd blocks with border patterns, patchwork or strips of printed fabric.

66 *English appliqué, 1851.* (Victoria & Albert Museum, London)

67 The Children's Menagerie Quilt, *C.1900, 188 × 158cm (74 × 62in).* (The American Museum in Britain, Bath)

The shapes of the animals and birds have been cut from plain solid colours and applied to *squares of printed cottons, patched together. Each square is partially quilted and many shapes are outlined in machine stitching. This gives a slightly padded effect. The eyes of the animals and other details are delicately hand embroidered.*

The Baltimore Bride

The Peace Embroidery, Sheila Page

Above, Snake mola

Below, Bird mola

Baby's hammock cloth from India *(The Greenwich Museum)*

Pillow case from Rajasthan

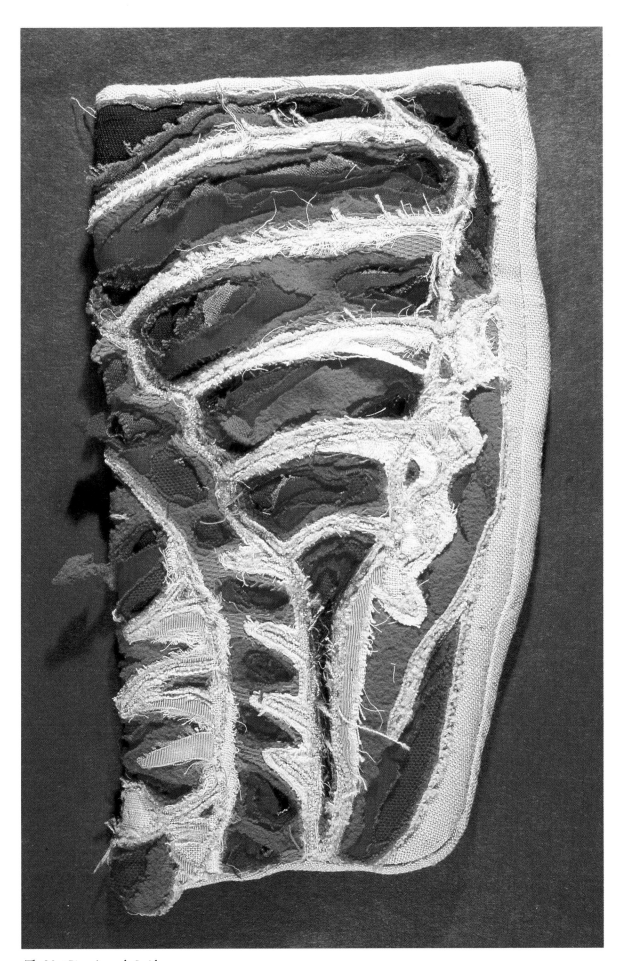

The Meat Piece, Amanda Smith

Silver Jubilee, Constance Howard

Detail of the *Silver Jubilee,* Constance Howard

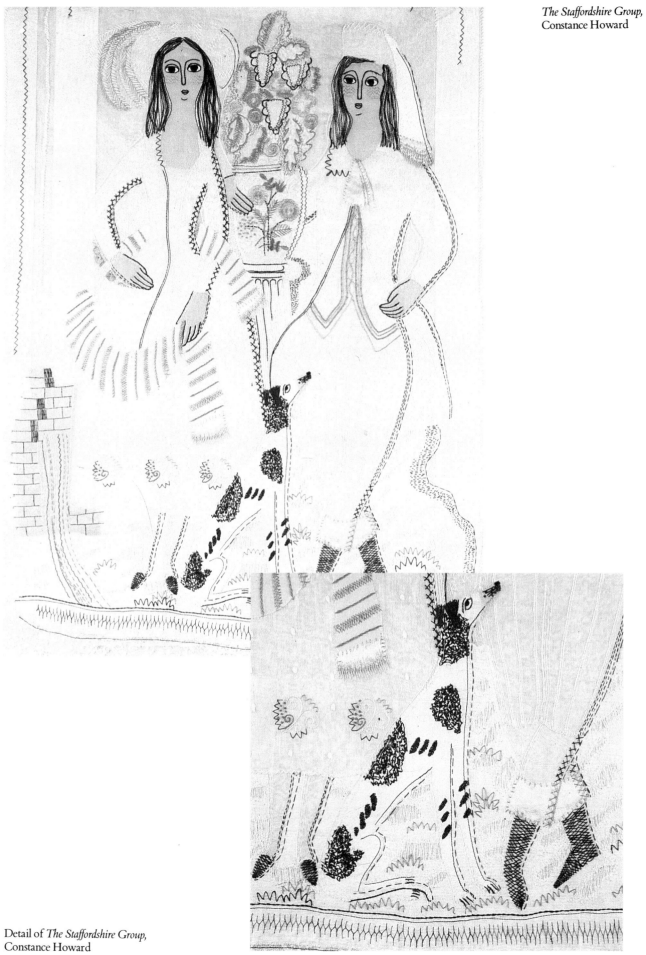

Detail of *The Staffordshire Group,*
Constance Howard

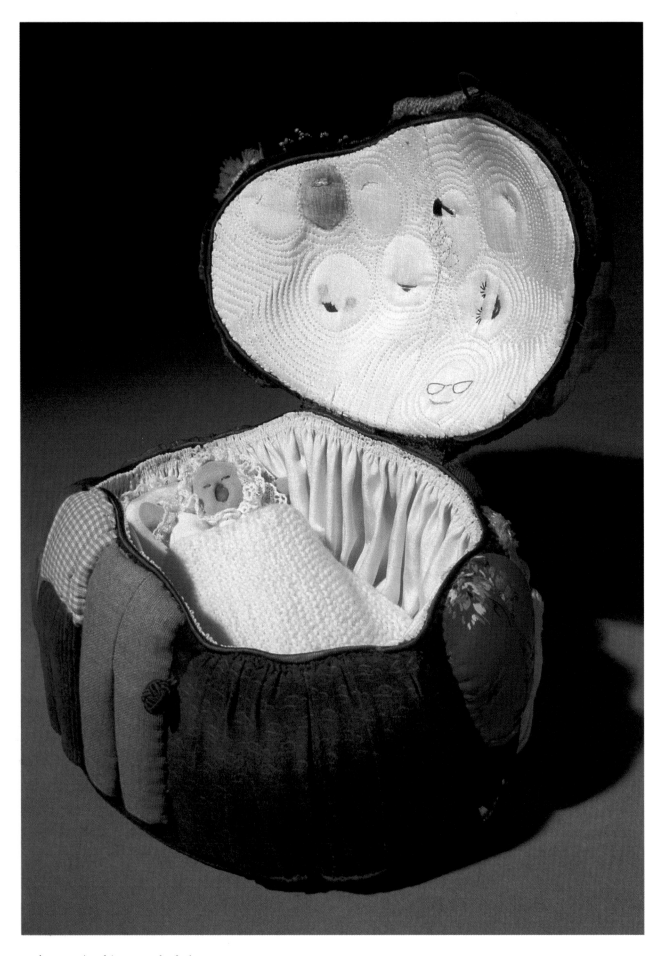

Little Precious (inside), Ann Rutherford

68 *Patterned fabrics.*

The appliqué panel in the Victoria & Albert Museum (fig. 66) demonstrates how the rhythm and pattern of printed fabrics can enhance silhouettes. Notice how the patterns of the printed cottons relate to the shape and movement of the animals, birds and figures. To discover the most effective relations between pattern and outline, scan over various printed fabrics through a card stencil of the shape (fig. 68) and compare the effect of patterns from different angles. The exact position of a pattern within an outline can be captured perfectly by drawing onto the fabric following the cut edge of the stencil.

EXTENSION IDEAS

As well as animals and birds, flowers, fruit and foliage, all sorts of everyday objects can be a source of design. Arrange simple cut-out shapes to build pictures. Telling a story through pictures and writing is fun and always very popular with children.

PROJECT 9
BOLDLY PATTERNED PRINTS FOR APPLIQUÉ

You will need:
- *a piece of plain fabric for a background*
- *a variety of boldy patterned printed cottons (washed and ironed)*
- *good quality sewing thread*
- *sharp, pointed embroidery scissors*
- *thin card, a cutting board and craft knife*
- *tracing paper and a pencil*

1 *Choose a design from design sheets 16, 17, or 18 or search through pictures and photographs for shapes with a strong silhouette and an uncomplicated outline.*

2 *Trace the outline of the design and transfer it onto thin card.*

3 *Then make a template and a stencil by cutting into the card with a craft knife, keeping the area surrounding the design intact.*

4 *Using the stencil as a view finder, scan over a variety of boldly patterned fabrics and search for interesting effects. Alter the angle of the view*

69 Nelson, Tigger and a Vase of Flowers, 24 × 22cm (9½ × 8in), pieced fabric appliquéd and quilted cotton, Janet Bolton.

The charm of Janet Bolton's appliqué lies in the directness of her images and the small scale and patterned fabrics she uses. Although the running stitches and complementary quilting give subtle textures and a special handsewn quality, these do not dominate the design. Each piece is ironed flat, like freshly ironed washing.

Janet's collection of fabrics is very important. These are mainly fine cottons and include the good fabric of washed worn clothes, striped and checked shirts, patterned fabrics subdued by dyes or bleaching, and interesting small prints. Her choice of fabric is very selective, and the scale of patterning, direction and quality of line, colour and tonal contrasts are finely balanced in her work. When sorting through her baskets of fabrics she finds the unexpected juxtaposition of prints a constant source of inspiration.

finder and explore the patterns in relation to the shape of the design. When a satisfying area of fabric has been found, draw an outline of the design using the stencil onto the right side of the fabric.

5 Cut out the shape allowing enough fabric for turnings.

6 Place the shape onto a background fabric with the straight grains matching.

7 Pin and tack within the outline allowing enough room for turnings.

8 Snip into corners and around curves to ease the fabric and to give a good line. Turn under the edges and hem.

EXTENSION IDEAS
The piece could be incorporated into the design of a garment or cushion. Strips of plain or patterned fabrics could be used to frame or extend the panel. Several small appliqué pictures made in this way could be pieced together and quilted. The patterned shapes could be applied to patterned background fabrics or over several different colours pieced together.

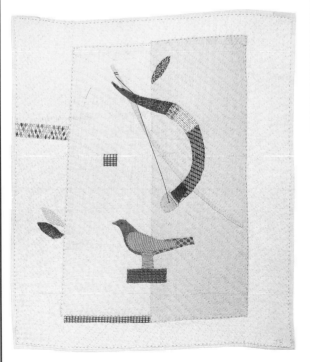

70 *Paper snake and bird, 50 × 50cm (20 × 20in), pieced fabric, appliquéd and quilted cotton, Janet Bolton.*

PROJECT 10
SPOTS, CHECKS AND STRIPES FOR APPLIQUÉ

You will need:
- a variety of fine printed cottons to give a lively mix of spots, checks and stripes. (The good cloth of worn clothing is ideal because it is free of dressing, colour-fast and pre-shrunk.) Wash new fabrics and iron all fabrics.
- sharp pointed embroidery scissors
- pins and a fine sharp needle

1 Sort through the fabrics and arrange them in compatible groups. Search for a lively combination of up to five fabrics. Select one fabric to be the background and choose the others to go with it. Consider varying proportions, juxtapositions and combinations.

2 Match sewing and embroidery threads to the fabrics. Add very small buttons and beads to the collection.

3 Choose a design from design sheets 16, 17 and 18. Make a template of it. Draw round the template to mark the design onto one of the fabrics. Then cut out the shape around the outline, allowing a little extra for turnings.

4 Pin the cut shape onto the background and look at the effect. Cut the same shape out in different fabrics and some new shapes from the design sheet.

5 Move and pin the different shapes together on the background until they settle into an interesting composition. Tack the motifs into place well within the outlines to allow for turnings.

6 Snip the cut edges to ease the curves and turn corners under with running stitch. Turnings should be small and close enough to hold the fabric without fraying, but their depth depends on the firmness of the fabric and the scale of the work. To cope with corners crease the fabric back across the points and fold under the edges. Begin stitching from the centre of the points then work along the rest of the shape.

7 When the appliqué is complete, quilt the whole piece with running stitch to hold the layers together.

EXTENSION IDEAS

Try extending or framing the design with strips of fabric and bind the raw edges. Several designs could be pieced together. These could be simply hung and enjoyed as pictures or become panels in a garment, cushion or quilt.

Appliqué is about shapes, areas of colour and patterning, so search for motifs with strong silhouettes. Look around you – a blackbird on the lawn, an apple on a checked cloth, a toy or objects on a shelf may form an interesting design. Try a simple line drawing, just the main shapes. This is not easy. It may take several attempts to achieve something pleasing but the effort will be rewarding.

71 *Nineteenth-century English patchwork quilt and appliqué, 280 × 280cm (110 × 110in) square. (Given by Miss J. I. Auty to the Victoria & Albert Museum)*

Notice the way in which ornate vases and flowers cut from chintz are combined with simple silhouettes cut from 'sprig and spot' prints. The formal arrangement of vases and bouquets follows the construction of the quilt with single leaves or smaller sprays to fill the spaces and to mask where the blocks join.

72 Tree of Life, *late eighteenth century chintz appliqué, 269 × 257cm (106 × 101in).* (The American Museum in Britain, Bath)

In this example, the best pieces of worn Indian chintzes or palampores have been applied onto a fine American homespun cotton. The diagonal quilting is typical of early quilts.

APPLIED CHINTZ

The word 'chintz' comes from the Indian for spotted cloth, 'chitta', applied to the cotton bed-spreads and hangings imported from India through the East India Trade Company which operated from the 1600s into the early nineteenth century. These cloths were woodblock printed or pencilled by hand using a split bamboo. A wad of hair or rag wrapped above the point held the dye until it was gently squeezed whilst drawing. The Indian cottons were brightly coloured, compara-tively cheap and washable – all fairly unusual qualities for fabric in seventeenth- and eighteenth-century Europe before textile printing on a large scale began.

Gradually, Indian and European designs united to make a cloth that was European in inspiration but unmistakably Indian in its total effect. Whilst the scrolls, scallops and plant forms were strongly influenced by Elizabethan design, the tree of life motif, peonies, chrysanthemums, carnations and exotic birds were oriental in origin. In chintz, palms are mixed with oaks, and pomegranates or pineapples grow from the same trees as apples and cherries. Pattern books containing all these elements were popular all over Europe, and designs were copied and adapted for different sorts of needlework.

Between the 1750s and the 1850s, block, pencil, and plate printing methods were developed in Holland, France and England. French block prints, influenced by Indian cottons, are known as *Indiennes*. It was the French copperplate printers who produced the famous *toile de Jouy*. Gradually these techniques were superseded by roller printing, which eventually made possible the mechanized mass production of cheap, printed cottons.

SABRINA WORK

Sabrina work consists of cutting whole flowers, single petals and leaves directly from coloured velvets and satins. These are lightly tacked onto a coloured background, often linen, and applied with widely spaced buttonhole stitch in matching thread. The flower centres are filled with french knots or satin stitch, and the stalks and tendrils worked in chain and stem with silk.

BRODERIE PERSE

Broderie perse is a combination of appliqué and embroidery in which figures and animals, trees and flowers and other motifs are cut out of printed fabrics, particularly Indian palampores (cotton bed covers) and chintzes, and applied onto a plain ground. Traditionally, the back of the chintz was covered with a paste to keep the fabric firm and pasted down onto the background fabric to hold them in place – the paste was washed out when the cover was washed. The intricately cut outlines were then covered with very fine blanket stitch, and the applied shapes were often filled with embroidered details and stems or tendrils embroidered in the spaces between the appliqué with stem and chain stitch. On many examples it is interesting to see how embroidery reasserts itself in decoratively coiling patterns.

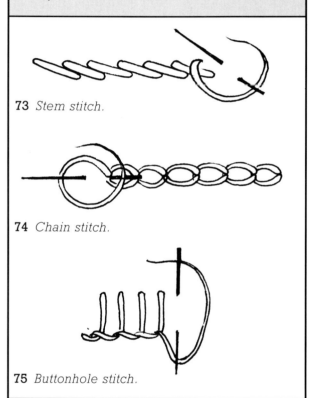

73 *Stem stitch.*

74 *Chain stitch.*

75 *Buttonhole stitch.*

SUGGESTED READING
Sheila Betterton. *American Textiles and Needlework.* The American Museum in Britain.

Sheila Betterton. *Quilts and Coverlets.* Reprinted by The American Museum in Britain, 1978, 1982.

Carleton L. Stafford and Robert Bishop. *America's Quilts and Coverlets.* Studio Vista London, 1972.

Beth Gutcheon. *The Perfect Patchwork Primer.* Penguin Books, 1973.

Robert Bishop. *New Discoveries in American Quilts.* E.P. Dutton and Co., 1975.

Thelma Newman. *Quilting, Patchwork, Appliqué and Trapunto.* George Allen and Unwin Ltd.

76 *A motif, 25 × 25cm (10 × 10in), Ann Ward, 1987.*

A motif, cut from a furnishing fabric printed to imitate stencil designs, applied onto calico with chain stitch in soft embroidery cotton. Notice the satisfying way in which the lines of chain stitch fill in the spaces. When the stitching is complete the appliqué will be slightly stuffed.

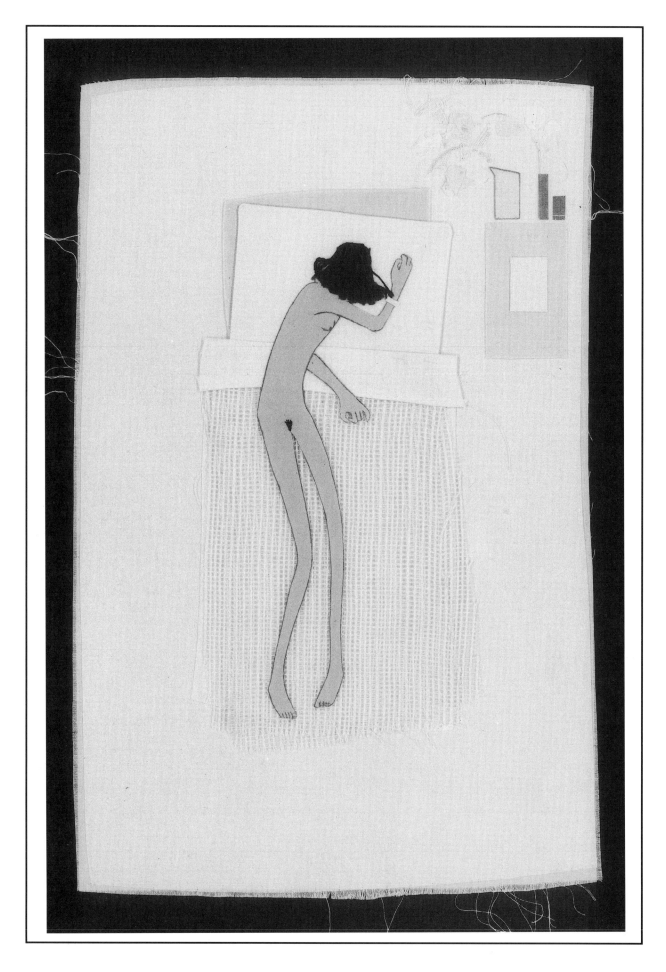

4 APPLYING BY BONDING

GENERAL TIPS

Bonding fabrics with iron-on interfacing or fusible fabric adhesive is an alternative to turning under the edges of applied shapes and prevents fraying. This can be helpful when applying intricate outlines and knitted or loosely woven fabrics, which can be very difficult to apply successfully because they stretch. Although their drape will be effectively stiffened, bonding them onto an iron-on interfacing or fusing them with the background before stitching will control this. Light coloured or white fabrics applied onto a dark ground are sometimes too transparent, and the strong background colour and hem turnings may show through. This can be remedied by fusing the light fabrics with white muslin or bonding them onto light weight iron-on interfacing. Any differences in varying weights of fabrics to be applied together can also be adjusted in this way. Ironing

with a damp pressing cloth will help to avoid puckering and ensure that the bonding does not come apart during washing. Remember, too much heat on certain synthetics can damage the fibres and fabric surface. Always test the temperature on a separate piece.

FUSIBLE FABRIC ADHESIVE

Fusible fabric adhesive comes on sheets of thin transparent paper. The rough side is the side that sticks. Place this on the wrong side of the fabric and bond by ironing from the smooth paper side. Then peel the paper away to leave a thin layer of adhesive on the wrong side of the fabric. Turn the fabric over and place it with the right side uppermost on the right side of the background fabric. They can then be bonded together with an iron through a damp cloth.

IRON-ON INTERFACING

Iron-on interfacing can be purchased in various weights to suit different fabrics and purposes. Again, it is the rough side that sticks. Place this on the wrong side of the fabric, rough side down, and bond from the smooth side of the interfacing by ironing, using a damp cloth.

Some iron-on interfacings are double sided and bond both the top fabric and background fabric to the interfacing simultaneously. These are sandwiched between two fabrics and bonded under the top fabric by ironing through a damp cloth.

Neaten the cut outlines of shapes bonded with iron-on facing and areas of fabrics fused to the background with zigzag or satin stitch machining. Although the fabrics become stiff and lose their flexibility and drape, iron-on interfacing and fusible fabric adhesives provide quick and effective

(Left:) **77** Hospital Corners, *60 × 34cm (24 × 17½in) Sheila Page.* (Courtesy of Roy and Dorothy Gillespie)

This piece was conceived as a result of a hospital visit some years ago. Sheila wanted to convey the cleanliness, the calm, white efficiency of a hospital ward and to express the vulnerability that she felt. The piece is worked in shades of cream and white on a grey background. The bed and the locker consist of pieces of cotton fabric frayed slightly at the edges, stiffened with spray starch. The pillow is slightly padded. The bed cover is a piece of net curtain. The figure was made by stiffening a fabric with iron-on interfacing, cutting it out and applying it directly. The raw edges are painted, not turned under. The details of the figure are either painted or stitched simply.

ways of keeping applied fabrics flat and secure during stitching and give a neat strong finish in which the layers are kept together without any additional stitching.

DESIGNING WITH INTERFACING

Transferring designs is clean and easy because you can freely draw or trace shapes around templates on the smooth side of the interfacing or paper backing of the fusible fabric adhesives. But remember to turn the image over to the reverse side beforehand, particularly with lettering, because in turning the fabrics over, images are all too easily cut the wrong way round.

A clear line drawing placed under a lightweight iron-on interfacing or fusible fabric adhesive can be traced directly onto them if held up against a sunny window or placed over a light-box. The tracing dispenses with templates and provides an ideal way of managing the practical problems of a composition made up of many interlocking pieces and different fabrics. Cut the traced design up and bond each shape onto an appropriate fabric. After any surplus fabric has been trimmed away the design pieces can be reassembled onto a copy of the drawing marked onto a background fabric, jigsaw fashion, the cut edges interlocking and butting up with one another.

Finally, secure and neaten the cut edges by zigzag or satin stitch machining but watch how these machine outlines relate to the design – the stitch width should be wide enough to bridge the join and stitch into neighbouring areas equally.

THE USE OF STARCH

When applying designs to clothing the stiffness associated with iron-on interfacing or fusible fabric adhesive may be undesirable or impractical. Flimsy or sheer fabrics such as chiffons, gauzy synthetics, nets and lawns are easier to apply if stiffened temporarily with starch. A spray or liquid starch will give a firm crisp edge to work with and wash out without spoiling the fabric or the drape of the garment. To do this spray starch on the wrong side of the fabric and cut out the pieces to be applied. Turn them over and place them on the background fabric and press with a warm iron through tissue paper. The pieces will stick down perfectly smooth and flat. Then secure and neaten the cut edges with zigzag or satin stitch machining. Wash out the starch afterwards and iron gently.

5 EMBROIDERY AND APPLIQUÉ

RESHT WORK

Persian in origin, resht work was used to decorate saddle cloths and prayer mats and covers for sofas or tables, particularly in the eighteenth and nineteenth centuries. Designs are created from an inlaid patchwork of different coloured wools. These are applied with silk threads, neatened with cords and chain stitch and decorated with gold threads and spangles.

There is a delightful but unusually small nineteenth century portrait of a dancing girl in resht work in the Victoria & Albert Museum. Larger versions of similar entertainers were set into niches of the Shah's palace in Teheran. Chequered chain stitch is often used in resht work.

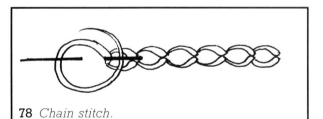

78 *Chain stitch.*

CHEQUERED CHAIN STITCH
For chequered chain stitch, the needle is threaded with two strands of different colours; each is used alternately to make a chain.

79 *Chequered chain stitch.*

COLLAGE AND STITCHES

When fabric pieces are assembled and pasted or simply tacked down rather than sewn together, this is a form of collage, from the French verb meaning 'to paste' or 'to glue'. Many of Christine Risley's early pieces are fabric collages with hand embroidery. *A Midsummer Fairy* (fig. 81) is a typical example of the experimental thinking current in the 1950s. In contemporary work, when we think of Richard Box's flower series and Christine Risley's machine-embroidered collages, it seems that collage, appliqué and embroidery are indivisible, particularly when machine techniques are also involved.

80 *Persian saddle cloth, eighteenth or nineteenth century resht work, 1.5 × 1.3m (5ft 2in × 4ft 3in). (Given by Mrs Hinchley to the Victoria & Albert Museum)*

Christine Risley's A Midsummer Fairy *is an example of fabric collage with hand embroidery. All the applied pieces were first tacked to the background and caught down with a small stitch, then embroidered with added beads and sequins. She never uses glue of any kind in her work because in time it tends to discolour the fabric.*

Many pieces of contemporary embroidery incorporate applied fabrics with stitch but perhaps it is the particular way in which design, fabric, construction and stitch are used together which differentiates appliqué from forms of embroidery, where applied fabrics simply provide background colour.

Many embroidery stitches are closely associated with appliqué. Couching, herringbone, and buttonhole for example, can be used to stitch down a shape, cover a raw edge and soften or emphasize an outline simultaneously. The colour and tone and width of an outline is important to get right. If the colour is matched too closely to either the applied shape or its background it will tend to increase the area of a shape and can make a considerable difference to the balance of a design. Strong, decoratively stitched outlines often feature inlay techniques where the raw edges of the fabrics are neatened and strengthened with various forms of couching.

Mary Thomas in her *Dictionary of Embroidery Stitches* lists stitches under different headings to suggest at a glance how they could be used. There are 35 possibilities under her heading for outline stitches! I think it is worth listing them for you. You may not be familiar with all of them but it would be worth while to look them up and learn to stitch some of the ones you do not know.

82 *Scroll stitch.*

83 *Twisted chain.*

84 *Coral knot stitch.*

85 *Fly stitch.*

86 *Feather stitch.*

OUTLINE STITCHES

Blanket stitch	Buttonhole stitch	Feather stitch
Back stitch	Double back stitch	Threadback stitch
Chain stitch	Cable stitch	Knotted cable stitch
Back stitched chain	Broad chain	Chequered chain
Heavy chain	Knotted chain	Twisted chain
Whipped chain	Coral	Holbein stitch
Outline stitch	Overcasting	Detached overcast
Running stitch	Whipped running	Rope stitch
Stem stitch	Whipped stem	Scroll stitch
Pekinese stitch	Portuguese knotted stem	Dot stitch
Pearl stitch	Double knot stitch	Satin couching
Cross stitch	Couching	

87 *Knotted buttonhole.*

88 The Triumph of Ariadne, *100 × 150cm (36 × 60in), Richard Box, 1973.*

The panel shows the ascension of Ariadne, guided by Dionysus, into heaven. She is surrounded by major gods and goddesses, who are arranged in a series of cameos in two arcs around the sun and moon.

When the composition was complete the whole design was drawn up to scale and copied to make a paper pattern. First, dark textured wools were cut to pattern pieces cut from the design. These were assembled onto a piece of sheeting and applied with zigzag machining run over the interlocking edges. Once the background pieces were in place the sheeting was stretched taut over a wooden frame. Then the areas of wool were overlaid in places by light bands of lace and beaded nets.

The figures, cut from silver and gold kid, are stab stitched in place over a foundation of felt. A very fine needle was used with nylon thread. As the punched and indented outline is unavoidable, it has been made into a positive feature. When applying leather it is important to stitch from well within the outlines, and not too closely or too tightly because the holes pierced in the leather tend to join up and develop into splits and cuts.

Lines of gold thread couched around or across the leather figures are used as a form of drawing to emphasise an outline or define a leg or an arm. This adds to the linear quality of the piece. Notice the way in which dark silhouettes alternate with light ones and vice versa, and the way in which strings of knots and beads or a particular fabric repeat again and again throughout the composition like an echo. This is one of Richard Box's favourite design devices.

89 Bird, *18 × 26cm (7 × 10in), Winsome Douglas, 1951. (Embroiderers' Guild Collection)*

This piece of appliqué was designed and worked by Winsome Douglas for the Needle-work Development Scheme when decorative bird designs were very popular. Shapes of white cotton have been applied on a blue linen background and the raw edges neatly turned under and invisibly hemmed. The outlines have then been decoratively embroidered with variations of blanket stitch and the applied shape filled with different patterns embroidered in white perle cotton. The stitches used include chain and rosette chain, coral knot and buttonhole, herringbone stitch, feather and fly, stem stitch and french knots.

Embroidery is very useful for enhancing the outline of an appliqué shape. An edge can be softened with feather stitch, broken with herringbone or cretan, decorated with pretty variations of blanket stitch, or strengthened with solid lines of closely worked buttonhole or machine satin stitch. Embroidery can give details too fine to be achieved in cut cloth – for example, the features on a face or lines to extend a point. Blocks of stitching can obscure parts of a shape or blank out a section of outline and can provide texture. Sometimes embroidery is worked freely across the applied surfaces of a design, integrating the shapes with the background, or used to draw together separate motifs. This can be seen in examples of broderie perse. Interesting changes in colour can be created by stitching over areas with patterns or textures in contrasting threads.

90 *Detail of* Silver Jubilee *(colour section). 195 × 120cm (76 × 48in), appliqué with embroidery, Constance Howard, 1977.* (Northampton Museum and Art Gallery)

The Society of Stained Glass Designers asked Constance Howard to do a piece of work for their exhibition in celebration of the Queen's Silver Jubilee in 1977. She was inspired by a window hung with jubilee flags in a street in Oxford. Without drawing, she worked from memory and cut out the figures, plant shapes and flags in plain and printed fabrics and coloured nets. She applied these onto a dark blue background with zigzag machining.

The shapes appear to glow within the red sash window frame and sombre brick walls. The light within and the illusion of glass is cleverly achieved through lengths of space-dyed wool, couched with red so that a series of red, blue and white lines set up contrasts and

colour vibrations as they run over the brightly-coloured applied shapes. She found that it was difficult at first to get this variegated thread to lie straight. The first line took her over three hours to get right but she discovered a knack and became faster and better as she worked on!

Notice the couched coloured wool around each flag. It both fixes the fabric and covers the raw edges. More elaborate and decorative couching is worked around the flower heads and to cover the edges of the crinkled velvet leaves, some of which are slightly stuffed. Blocks of straight stitching on the plain areas of green help to bring the window box shapes forward or bridge the space between the flowers and the window by suggesting shadows. All in all this bold image, with its illusions of light and space, has been created through an economical but effective combination of machine appliqué and hand embroidery.

91 and **92** *Detail of the* Staffordshire Group *(colour section),* Constance Howard, 1956. *(Collection of Leicestershire County Council Schools' Service)*

Constance Howard's Staffordshire Group *beautifully demonstrates the use of embroidered outlines and patterning. The design was inspired by a Staffordshire figurine and a china dog. Strips of transparent pink and apricot fabrics are applied with zigzag and straight stitch machining. These establish a space which contains the group. A border of lace, a band of cretan stitch and a double layer of darned organdie suggest the ground. The two figures are essentially silhouettes, cut out from dotted and plain organdie, onto which the main design lines are drawn in white machine stitching with hand-stitched details. These are balanced with straight and zigzag rows of machining in black thread and rows of black running stitch and herringbone. These suggest shadows and form in a very direct but delicately decorative way. Notice how the patterning on the hats suggest form and shape. The dog is another silhouette cut in silk and applied with black and white lines of stitching; he is patterned with patches of free machine embroidery and lozenges of cretan stitch. Notice the way in which the diversity of these patterns and the strong tonal contrasts establish the dog in the front of the group and the subtle way in which the differences in outlines and details throughout the piece appear to make shapes overlap – thus creating form and space within and through embroidered lines and patterning.*

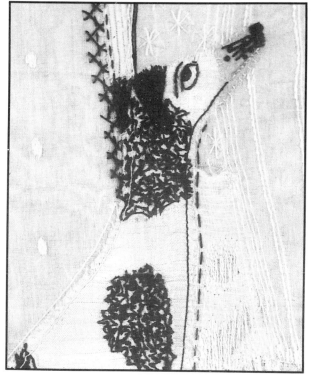

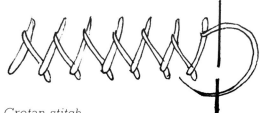

93 *Cretan stitch.*

(Left:) **94** The Magic Garden, *52 × 36cm (20½ × 14½in), Rebecca Crompton, 1895–1947.* (Victoria & Albert Museum, London)

*Rebecca Crompton through her teaching and embroidery encouraged a free approach and spontaneous expression. She wrote, 'Embroidery should never look as though it were squeezed out of shape in order to follow a precious conception of correct drawing or illustration . . . as the fancy moves us we can vary the detail of our repeating patterns in any way and at any time.' (*Modern Design in Embroidery*, B.T. Batsford Ltd, 1939)*

Notice the way her embroidery fills areas with patterns and travels across shapes.

95 The Peace Embroidery *(colour section), 200 × 270cm (78 × 106in), Sheila Page.* (Dundee CND)

The Peace Embroidery came about as a result of a competition organized by Dundee CND in 1984 to design an embroidery to commemorate the fortieth anniversary of the dropping of the atom bomb on Hiroshima in 1945. Paper designs were submitted in June 1984, and the winner had one year in which to complete the work. The theme was based on some lines from Pope John Paul II's speech in Hiroshima:

> To remember the past is to commit oneself to the future. To remember Hiroshima is to abhor nuclear war. To remember Hiroshima is to commit oneself to peace.

The design begins with a mushroom cloud in the top left hand corner and progresses downwards with falling interlocking figures and other images of devastation. The cloud was made by covering a Vilene (Pellon) shape. The figures were made by machine-edged appliqué with some strong, simple stitchery. This gives a good, sombre-coloured integrated surface. From the scene of devastation some more hopeful symbols begin to emerge – roots, stems and flowers. These progress upwards to the right-hand area to a golden city in the centre of the piece. There are flags of all the nations and a hillside covered with peaceful images of cows, crops and flowers. This section is very brightly-coloured to contrast with the first section.

The applied fabrics are light-weight cottons, polycotton sheeting, viyella and some silk, so that the final piece is not too heavy. Each section was applied in turn. Finally the whole piece was stretched over a huge frame.

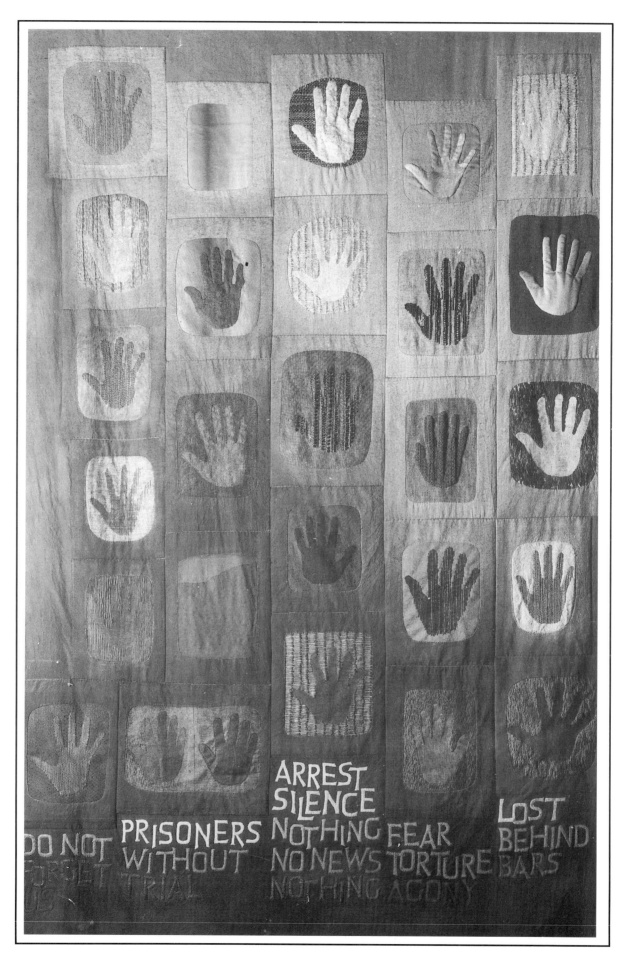

(Left and below:) **96** Prisoners of Conscience, *300 × 180cm (118 × 70in), Audrey Ormond, 1978. (All* Hallows-by-the-Tower, City of London)

There are said to be over 100,000 prisoners of conscience in the world, imprisoned without trial. Audrey Ormond had unsuccessfully struggled to depict the prisoners' agony and fear in an embroidery, until she saw a photograph of the imprints of an Indian woman's hands pressed into soft plaster before she threw herself onto the funeral pyre of her husband. The life size hands of many men and women are framed within the hanging. Some of the hands are stitched and some applied. The prison bars are echoed in lines of embroidery. The two empty spaces are left to provoke thought.

The panel is worked in a variety of techniques. Most of the fabrics and threads are dyed in sombre colours and chosen to give a rough effect. The lettering is cut out in fine leathers and applied in a bold way with matching thread.

APPLIQUÉ FOR LARGE SCALE WORK

Appliqué covers large areas relatively quickly and economically. It concerns broad surfaces of fabric and clear cut images which read effectively from a distance. For these reasons it is an ideal technique for banners and wall hangings, lecterns and altar frontals, ceremonial or eye-catching clothing and accessories.

The most effective forms of appliqué are very often simply designed, particularly if the work is intended to be viewed across a large room, perhaps in a foyer or church. The wall hanging in All Hallows-by-the-Tower, made by **Audrey Ormond**, is a powerful and moving example (fig. 96). Although well balanced areas of colour and the choice of fabrics are the most important ingredients of good appliqué, in many historical and contemporary pieces embroidery and appliqué are often beautifully combined. The stitching need not be immediately apparent – after the initial impact of the work, embroidery provides a second level of visual interest and enjoyment when the piece is seen close to.

SUGGESTED READING

Mary Thomas. *Dictionary of Embroidery Stitches.* Hodder and Stoughton, 1934 and 1985 (paperback).
Constance Howard and Christine Risley. *Eirian Short Exhibition Catalogue.* University of London, Goldsmiths College, Department of Textiles, 1985.
Mrs Archibald Christie. *Stitches and Samplers.* B.T. Batsford Ltd, 1920 and 1985 (paperback).
Anne Butler. *The Batsford Encyclopaedia of Embroidery Stitches.* B.T. Batsford Ltd, 1979.
The Constance Howard Book of Stitches. B.T. Batsford Ltd, 1979.
Evangeline Shears and Diantha Fielding. *Appliqué.* Pitman Publishing, London; Watson-Guptill Publications, New York, 1972.
Margot Carter Blair and Cathleen Ryan. *Banners and Flags: how to sew a celebration.* Harcourt Brace Jovanovich, 1977.

6 DESIGNING THROUGH PAPER: CUT-OUTS AND COLLAGE

Design for appliqué is about colour, shape and space. Shapes within a design can be placed apart from one another in isolated patches. Whether isolated, detached, interlocking, overlapping or layered, the shapes have to be practical to cut out and sew. For the shapes used in appliqué, the edges of smooth gentle curves, straight lines and open angles are easier to turn under and sew down successfully than complicated outlines and narrow points. It is always worthwhile, before beginning any piece of work, to test your fabrics and threads. To achieve a satisfying result the design, the fabrics, the needle and thread, and the character of the stitching should be right. It will soon become apparent on the test piece if a design needs to be adjusted or simplified, or one aspect needs changing.

DRAWING AND TRACING

Try making the shapes of birds and animals, flowers, figures, objects and architecture in simple, clear outlines. With practice, you can design directly from the world about you. Any design is possible so long as it is expressed in a strong simple way with clear bold outlines. Books and magazines are full of appealing pictures which are possible to adapt and trace. A design can be scaled up by using squared paper (fig. 97) or enlarged on a photocopier.

STENCILS AND TEMPLATES

Paper cut-outs, card stencils or templates, and collage can all help to bridge the gap between ideas and appliqué techniques. Exploring and planning designs through cutting out and arranging shapes in paper not only provide patterns but also suggest the order in which to work them and the most appropriate techniques to use.

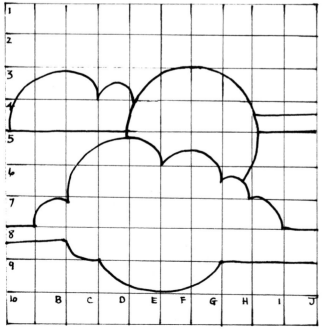

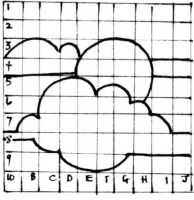

97 *A design can be scaled up using graph paper.*

FOLDED AND CUT-OUT SHAPES

Ideas for appliqué can be based on folded and cut-out shapes. Cutting into folded paper is a very direct and inexpensive way of creating interesting patterns (see figs 18 and 19) and linked chains of doll or animals. Some of these will be simple, others very intricate, but remember that the more complicated outlines are difficult to apply unless they are cut and worked on a very large scale, as quilt designs are in Hawaii (see fig. 26). Transferring the design is simply a matter of folding the fabric in exactly the same way, and making the same cuts in the same places.

USE OF A VIEW FINDER

The appliqué panel in the Victoria & Albert Museum (fig. 66) demonstrates how the rhythm and pattern of printed fabrics can enhance the silhouette. To discover the most effective relationship between pattern and outline, scan over various printed fabrics through a card stencil of the shape (fig. 68) and compare the effect of patterns from different angles. The exact position of a pattern within an outline can be captured perfectly by drawing onto the fabric within the stencil around the cut edge of card. Remove the stencil and cut the shape out allowing 1cm (⅜in) of extra fabric all the way round for turnings, unless the shape is to be applied by machining.

Printed fabrics can be photocopied and cut up to compose a design. This is an invaluable way of testing different combinations of prints or design ideas before cutting into precious fabrics.

PLANNING

The applied birds and animals in the *Children's Menagerie* (fig. 67) and the figures in the piece at the Victoria & Albert Museum, are isolated shapes whereas, the stencil-like shapes in *The Baltimore Bride* overlap in places (fig. 63). This effect is reinforced by the differences in tone value between the yellows and reds or yellows and blues. Coloured paper is very helpful for planning a design in which shapes overlap and complicated linear drawings seem confusing. Coloured papers not only help to differentiate shapes in overlapping designs but also represent different coloured fabrics and order of work. The shapes for a design can be revised and arranged again and again with more shapes added until a satisfying composition is achieved. This may combine both overlapping shapes and isolated motifs. Templates can be made for all the shapes required to transfer the design onto the fabrics.

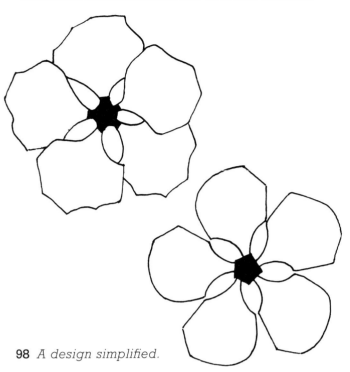

98 *A design simplified.*

TRANSFERRING THE DESIGN

It may be helpful to make a tracing of a design composed of lots of shapes by outlining all the shapes through tissue paper and to transfer the tracing onto the background fabric by tacking through the tissue following the outlines. Use different coloured thread to indicate different coloured shapes. When the outlines are completed tear the tissue paper away. Number the areas in the order in which they should be applied.

COLOUR AND TEXTURE

Working through coloured paper cut-outs and collage allows you to explore colours. The three primary colours, red, yellow and blue, read most clearly from a distance, particularly on a background of white or black. Many appliqué pieces, therefore, rely on various combinations of yellow, red, blue and green, and orange and violet. Alternatively, strong contrasts of light and dark colours are used. Colours need not, however, be over-bright or garish. Good quality coloured papers are very expensive. It is is possible to make your own paper and to stain paper with dyes to match dyed fabrics. You can also colour paper with gouache paint, water colours, water-proof inks, wax crayons, etc. and it is worthwhile collecting a whole range of different papers with interesting patterns and textures. The qualities of different papers can correspond with certain fabrics, for example, corrugated paper with corduroy, tissue paper with silk organza.

7 TRANSFERRING A DESIGN

GENERAL TIPS

Whenever possible, cut shapes in fabric so that the design runs straight with the grain of the fabric. Apply them with the straight grain matching the straight grain of the background fabric. This keeps the work flat and helps to prevent puckering. Careful attention to the structure or weave of the fabric can perfect the constructional and textile quality of a piece of appliqué (fig. 99). To match the grains mark the horizontal or vertical with a straight arrow on each paper pattern or template. Align this with the straight grain of the fabric when the shape is transferred.

There are several ways of transferring a design. If the fabric to be applied is thin enough, the design can be traced directly through the cloth using a transfer pen, chalk, or pencil. Hold the work up against a sunlit window or over a light-box to help.

A design can be transferred by tacking through lines traced onto tissue paper. When the tacking is complete, slit the tissue under each stitch with a needle. Then lift the tracing gently away, leaving the lines of tacking on the fabric (different coloured threads may help to clarify the shapes or indicate overlaps). This is a suitable way of transferring designs onto delicate wools or silks. For fabrics with a pile, such as velvet, place and tack the tracing through from the wrong side.

THE 'PRICK AND POUNCE' METHOD

The 'prick and pounce' method is a suitable way of transferring outlines onto smooth fabrics, such as linens, satins or silks.

☆ Trace the design onto transparent paper.

☆ Place the tracing on two thicknesses of blanket with a piece of tissue paper between the tracing paper and the blanket.

☆ Closely prick along all the lines with a needle.

☆ Position the pricking on the fabric and hold it in place with some weights.

☆ Rub through a 'pounce' of powdered tailor's chalk and/or charcoal with a small round pad.

☆ Take off the weights. Carefully lift off the tracing, then the tissue. Gently blow away any surplus powder.

☆ Then, using a fine sable brush, link the dots with a line of pale blue water colour paint. Alternatively, use black or white oil paint thinned with turpentine.

OTHER METHODS

Designs are often marked out around a template or stencil with a fine, hard pencil but the graphite tends to come off on the sewing thread or to leave permanent marks on the fabric. Tailor's chalk is useful for dark or patterned fabrics and water-soluble transfer pens are also available. These pens leave turquoise lines, which on most fabrics disappear as if by magic on contact with water or steam. Sometimes the lines reappear as the fabric dries and may need re-wetting several times. The pens are not suitable for all fabrics because they can leave stubborn, yellow marks, so always test them out first.

Draw a design onto patterned drafting paper to make a paper pattern. Cut out the paper shapes and pin these onto the fabrics and cut around them. Alternatively, use a photocopier to enlarge or reduce designs.

A copy of the design composed of lots of shapes and different fabrics can be cut up to make patterns for all the various pieces. Pin each pattern onto a fabric and cut it out in turn. The different fabric shapes are then re-assembled and applied. It can be helpful to mark out the whole of the design onto a background fabric. Put the separate pieces into place quickly and accurately. You can do this by making a tracing of the whole design onto tissue paper and transferring the tissue following the outlines. Different coloured threads can be used to indicate different shapes. When the outlines are complete, gently tear the tissue away. The areas can be numbered in the sequence the shapes are to be applied.

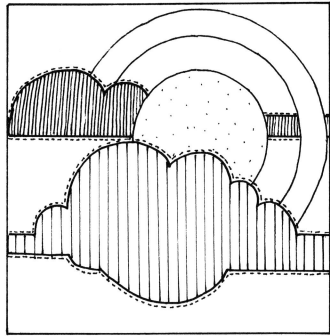

100 *Design composed of overlapping shapes.*

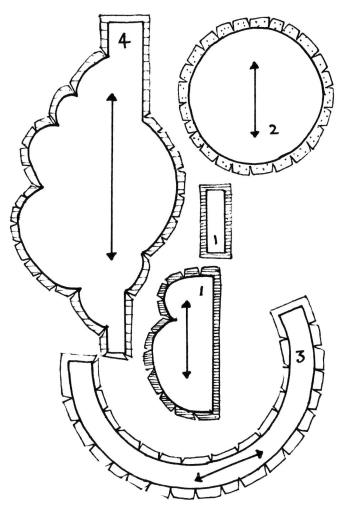

99 *Marking the straight grain*

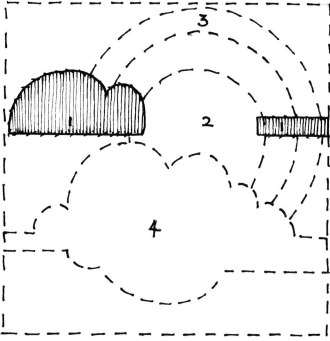

101 *Design composed of lots of shapes matched with tacking onto the background.*

8 MACHINE EMBROIDERY

YOUR MACHINE

Zigzag machining provides a comparatively fast and effective way of securing and neatening applied shapes. When zigzag stitches are machined closely together they form a solid line of satin stitch. This takes up a great deal of thread. Satin stitch gives a smooth, very well defined outline, particularly appropriate for appliqué on articles expected to be washed frequently because the stitches completely encase the raw edges. To achieve a really even outline, the needle should be fine and always very sharp; an open-toed foot is also helpful.

Vary the stitch width and length without stopping the machine by simply moving the settings, so a whole range of linear differences can be achieved in a continuous line of stitching. Four or five set embroidery patterns are built into some machines, while fully automatic machines may have up to 20 or more.

By removing the pressure foot, and covering or lowering the feed plate, machining is not even restricted to straight lines. The fabric can be moved in any direction. In order to do this, stretch the fabric in a ring frame. The ring can be moved freely to and fro and the stitching follows the movement of the ring. In this way series of circles, very intricate patterns, and patches of texture can be created.

Successful machine appliqué depends on a well-adjusted, smooth-running machine and good machine skills. Use the right needle and good quality thread too – poor quality thread tends to break readily, and uneven stitching is frequently caused by blunt or bent needles. It is worth settling down with your machine and its instruction manual just to explore the range of possibilities it has to offer.

Always check the thread and stitch tension by sewing on a test piece which corresponds exactly to the fabrics to be used.

For zigzag and satin stitch loosen the top tension slightly so that the stitches interlock underneath both pieces of fabric. On the wrong side of the work the bobbin thread should appear as a narrow zigzag running between the top thread.

Very closely machined satin stitch tends to pull inwards, distorting the fabric. To counter this, spread the fabric taut with your fingers in a V-shape on either side of the pressure foot as you feed the fabric through.

Thread thicknesses vary from buttonhole twist to average thickness (40), fine (50), very fine (60). Machine embroidery thread can be fine (30) or very fine (50).

There are different types of needles to suit different purposes, for example, ballpoints, leather needles, jean needles, twin needles. Sizes vary as follows: very fine; fine; average; for heavy fabrics; for very heavy duty sewing.

MANOEUVRING AROUND CURVES, CORNERS AND POINTS

It is worth practising and mastering manoeuvring the machine around curves, corners and points. Uncertain machining can spoil the overall quality of machine appliqué, whereas perfectly controlled stitching can give a superb finish to a piece.

FABRICS	THREADS	SPECIAL REQUIREMENTS
Transparent fabrics: organza, chiffon, voile georgette, muslin	Mach, Em,. 50	Use small open zigzag with two fabrics stretched together in a ring frame. Free machine in a ring frame. Straight stitch through paper which is torn away afterwards.
Nets	Mach, Em, 50 Cotton 40	Machine nets in a ring frame. Pull net taut little by little so as not to distort the weave.
Delicate fabrics: lawn, baptiste, chiffon, georgette, silk	Cotton 50 or 60 Mach, Em, 50 Silk	
Lightweight synthetics: sheer, gauzy organzas	Rayon Mach, Em, Synthetic	
Lightweight cottons:	Cotton 50 Mach, Em, 30	
Lightweight woollens:	Silk 40	
Firm, medium-weight silk	Silk 40	
Firm, medium-weight cotton: furnishing fabrics	Cotton 40	
Thick cottons: damasks	Cotton 40	
Heavy synthetics	Synthetic	
Very heavy weaves: mattress ticking, awning canvas, close denim	Cotton 40	
Embroidery canvas: linen, cotton, synthetic, plastic	Linen Cotton Synthetic	Set the machine to zigzag to cover or a number of threads in the weave.
Knits, soft, pliable, and very stretchy fabrics		Guide without pulling and distorting, gently spread the fabric out as it is fed under the pressure foot.
Synthetic fur fabrics	Synthetic	To create a smooth edge push fur away from the stitching as the fabric is fed under the pressure foot.
Fabrics with a pile: velvet, velour, corduroy	Cotton	Sometimes these fabrics require stitching twice to completely cover the cut pile. Machine the first outline with open zigzag. Trim. Then machine over the first line with a slightly larger, closer zigzag.
Gold and silver lamé	Metallic High sheen rayon	Use a plain thread in the bobbin. The top tension may need adjusting. Vibration can make this slippery thread slide down the reel and around the spool pin causing the thread to break. Work on a firm surface at a very even speed. Use a plain thread in the bobbin. The top tension may need adjusting.
Tinsel and lurex braids	Metallic High sheen rayon	See above.
Shiny fabrics: rayons, synthetic satins	Rayon, Mach, Em.	
Leather, suedes, cloth-backed plastics		Very close stitching will tend to split and cut leathers. Use a long straight stitch machined well within an outline, or use an open zigzag.
Plastic	Mercerized	Some plastics can be difficult to feed through the machine. A roller, a pressure foot, or a darning foot can be helpful. Use a long straight stitch or open zigzag. Sew slightly rounded rather than square corners.
Transparent acetates	High sheen rayon Mach, Em, 50	Long straight stitches or open zigzag

Stitching is turned on a curve corner or point by lifting the foot, leaving the needle down and pivoting the fabric. When machining with zigzag or satin stitch it is possible to pivot when the needle is on the right- or left-hand side of the stitching. Pivoting while the needle is on wrong side leaves gaps in the stitching. Pivoting when the needle is on the correct side creates a solid line of even stitches.

CURVES *(fig. 102)*

To achieve a good line, pivot whenever the needle begins to go out of line. Pivot frequently.

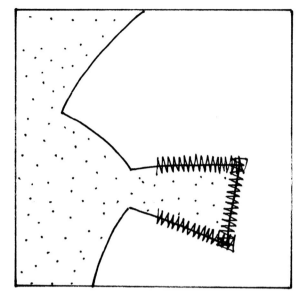

103 *Machine-stitched corners.*

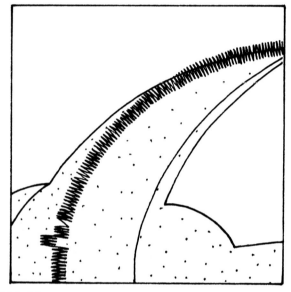

102 *Machine-stitched curves.*

CORNERS *(fig. 103)*

Stitch until the needle goes off the point of the corner. Pivot and continue along the next edge so that the stitches overlap on the corner. To prevent the stitching stacking up and blocking the machine after pivoting, stop and raise the pressure foot and needle. Move the fabric on a little. Drop the pressure foot again and continue.

POINTS *(fig. 104)*

Stitch along the edge until the needle comes off the fabric in its left hand swing. To stop a curve forming, pivot the fabric to bring the point into the centre of the pressure foot. Then, gradually decrease the width of the stitch to follow the narrowing point of the fabric. By the end of the point the stitch width should be on zero. Pivot and stitch out of the point by increasing the stitch width over the stitches just worked, back to the raw edge and the original stitch width. It may be helpful to mark the stitch setting on the machine with a piece of masking tape.

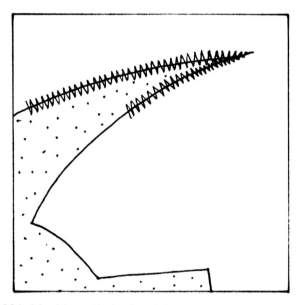

104 *Machine-stitched points.*

INVERTED ANGLES
(fig. 105)

Stitch along the edge to the end of the point. Continue stitching as far as the width of the stitching. Stop with the needle in the fabric on its left-hand swing. Pivot and continue stitching along the next edge. Allow the stitching to overlap inside the point. Do not leave a gap or the point will fray.

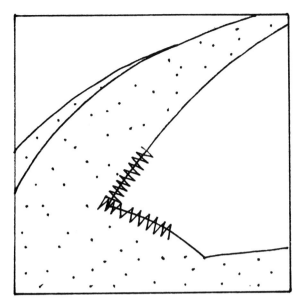

105 *Machine-stitched inverted angles.*

LINES OF STITCHING

Machine appliqué need not be limited to stitching around outlines.

Cut a shape of fabric and place it on a different background. Pin or tack or bond it into position and then run lots of lines of straight stitching across the area vertically, horizontally or at a slant. The thread could be cut at the end of each line or the stitching turned in various ways for the return journey.

EXTENSION IDEAS

Criss-cross lines to form grids and change thread colour. Variegated or metallic machine-embroidery threads are effective with transparent or gauzy fabrics. Beautiful surfaces can be created by machining across fabrics with interesting textures, for example, knitted fabrics, velvets, corduroys and satins.

PROJECT 11
TAKE A LINE OF ZIGZAG STITCHING FOR A WALK

You will need:
- *a piece of plain fabric approximately 25 × 25cm (10 × 10in)*
- *suitable thread*
- *swing needle sewing machine*
- *machine instruction manual*
- *small pair of sharp, pointed scissors*

1 Thread up the machine.

2 Set the stitch for a fairly close zigzag.

3 Check that the tension is correct on a small test piece cut from the same fabric.

4 Transfer a line similar to the one on design sheet 20 onto the fabric.

5 Place the fabric under the pressure foot.

6 Lower the foot. With the needle in the fabric on the line at start, begin stitching.

7 Follow the line to 'finish'.

8 Then continue in your own way.

INTRICATE OUTLINES

This method is suitable for lightweight, closely woven fabrics and materials which do not fray.

Select two fabrics and thread to match. Choose a design in which the positive and negative shapes are well balanced and the outlines enclose the areas to be applied or cut away. Draw the design up to the size required and transfer it onto the right side of the fabric to be applied. Having selected and tested the stitch length, place the fabric to be applied onto the second fabric with straight grain matching. Pin and tack them securely together to keep both pieces straight and flat. Machine around the design, pivoting carefully around curves and corners, then cut away the surplus areas.

EXTENSION IDEAS

Cut edges that have not been neatened can be a special feature and give softer outlines. Some fabrics, including gauzy synthetics and silks, fray beautifully. These can be overlaid onto other fabrics to create subtle colour changes and diffused edges. Shapes cut out with pinking shears will have lively, interesting outlines.

106 City Scapes, *Sharon Baker, 1986.*

Sharon Baker wants people to be aware of what is going on around them and to question a system which she feels cares little about people or the planet. As a student at Goldsmith's College, she found it difficult at first to translate her charcoal drawings into textiles. She overcame this by drawing directly with the machine, using fabrics for their own qualities. She incorporates masses of separate bits of fabrics and all kinds of materials including newspaper cuttings and printed propoganda onto large areas of applied calico, muslin and striped black and white ticking. In a series of cut, patched and layered fabric, landscapes, pylons and houses began to portray the forces of good and evil. They eventually became manic city scapes in which humanity, houses and cars are under layers of pressure from various forms of control and technology.

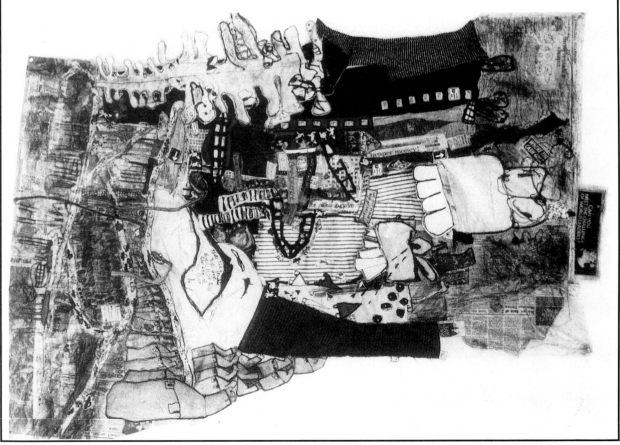

107 'This is a cat', *29 × 22cm (11½ × 8½in), Laura Boyd, 1985. (Courtesy of Guy Campbell)*

Laura Boyd first became interested in machine appliqué at Jordan Stone College of Art, Dundee. For this piece she backed scraps of cotton, lining fabrics and silk batiks, with iron-on interfacing to make it easier to cut out shapes without the fabric fraying. She tacked all the cut shapes into place onto a background fabric and then, with the machine set for a very short stitch length, zigzagged around, achieving a perfectly flat finish. For the line that upset the vase, she splashed the image with watery white gouache paint. When dried this created the ringed splash marks. Details on the face of the cat are painted with a thicker gouache.

108 *Detail of a cushion cover, c.1900, Jessie R Newberry. (Victoria & Albert Museum, London)*

Linen flowers are applied in shades of green and pink silk with satin stitch onto linen. The cover is bordered with needle weaving in green, cream and pink silks on drawn threads.

At the Glasgow School of Art, Jessie Newberry developed appliqué and embroidery techniques to creat distinctive designs in an Art Nouveau style.

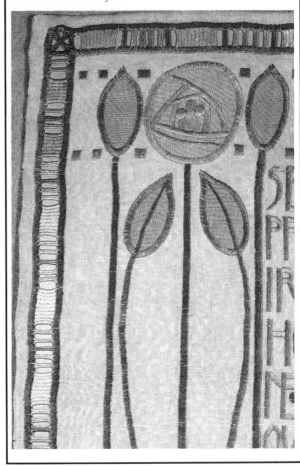

ZIGZAG AND SATIN STITCH

There are several different ways of applying fabrics with zigzag or satin stitch, depending on the fabrics and design. To help prevent puckering work with pre-shrunk, ironed cloth, cut the fabric shapes with the straight grain and apply them to the background fabric with the straight grain matching. When two or more applied shapes are wanted on top of one another the largest shape must be applied first on the bottom layer. If only one colour is used all the applied shapes can be neatened with a continuous line of stitching so long as the direction of the outline still relates to the design. If the shapes are outlined in different colours, each shape will have to be neatened in turn. Remember, where shapes overlap some edges will be hidden. A contrasting colour outline can appear to broaden or reduce the area of the design. Usually the colour of the thread is matched to the colour of the fabric, or sometimes a shade or two darker.

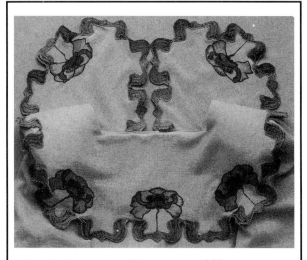

109a *Collar, Jean Chisholme, 1987.*

The design of this collar is strongly Art Nou-
veau. The motif was drawn from a glazed tile,
and the flowers and leaves are cut from painted
silk and applied with a machine.

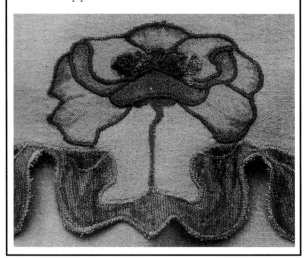

BASIC ZIGZAG

This method is suitable for appliqué pictures and
cotton fabrics. Decorative embroidery stitches
could be used.

☆ Cut out a fabric shape.

☆ Tack it onto the background fabric with the
tacks well within the outline or bond the shape
into place.

☆ Set the machine for an open zigzag.

☆ Start the stitching along a straight edge or
gentle curve, and machine around the outline
covering the raw edge.

TWO FABRICS TOGETHER

This method is suitable for designs applied to
garments. It is strong and all the raw edges are
encased within the stitching.

☆ Transfer a design onto the fabric to be applied.

☆ Place the fabric to be applied with the background fabric with the right sides up and the
straight grain matching.

☆ Tack inside the shapes well within their outlines.

☆ In a different colour, tack around the outer edge
of the fabrics to hold them together.

☆ Machine around the outlines of the design with
straight stitching.

☆ Trim away the fabric not required close to the
stitching.

☆ Then cover both the straight stitching and the
raw edge with close zigzag or satin stitch.

109b *Appliqué designed by Godfrey Blunt. (Vic-*
toria & Albert Museum, London)

EXTENSION IDEAS
The idea of machining fabrics together and then cutting one away can be explored by putting together unusual combinations, such as printed silks on fur fabrics, dyed muslins on handmade felt, felt on leather. The top fabric need not be entirely cut away. Shapes could be slashed and channels in layers of fabrics between lines of stitching ripped open.

LINES OF ZIGZAG

Zigzag stitch need not be limited to machining around outlines. If you arrange strips or fragments of fabrics on a sheet of fabric transfer adhesive and bond these onto a background fabric, you can then machine along or across the strips.

EXTENSION IDEAS
These strips could be torn or cut or pinked. The combination of different colours, textures and patterning in the applied fabrics produces some interesting textures and visually exciting effects. A variety of stitch widths and lengths could be combined with surface embroidery (fig. 110).

110 *Detail of Herbaceous Border at Parham, 38 × 25cm (15 × 10in), Vicky Lugg, 1986. (Courtesy of Anne Coleman)*

111 *Shoulder bag, 28 × 25cm (11 × 10in), Judith van der Weegen-Gussin, 1986.*

This shoulder bag is made in cotton furnishing fabric with canvas work. Notice the patch to strengthen the construction, and the detached leaves.

DETACHED SHAPES
(figs 111 and 112)

☆ Draw a shape onto a fabric, or onto one of two fabrics placed with their wrong sides together.

☆ Set the machine to an open zigzag.

☆ Start stitching along a straight edge or gentle curve.

☆ Complete the outline.

☆ Then trim the unwanted fabric away very close to the stitching.

☆ To neaten the edge cover the first line of stitching with close zigzag or satin stitch.

EXTENSION IDEAS
Before the unwanted fabric is trimmed away machine fine details and textures using free stitching. Some knitted and stretchy fabrics zigzag-stitched and pulled slightly in the machining will create beautifully fluted edges.

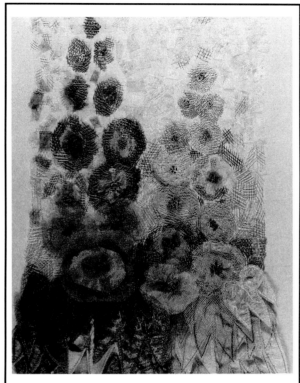

112 Delphiniums, *Sheila Gussin, 1987.*

Detached shapes can be used to make a variety of very effective leaves and flowers, which when attached together and applied can give a three dimensional form of appliqué.

Freely-machined shapes worked on vanishing muslins can be cut and applied in this way (fig. 112).

PLIABLE AND STRETCH FABRICS

For pliable and stretchy fabrics use a ballpoint needle.

☆ Transfer the design onto the fabric to be applied.

☆ Place this right side up onto the background fabric.

☆ Tack inside the shapes well within the outlines.

☆ Machine around the shape with an open zigzag.

☆ Trim away the surplus fabric close to the stitching.

☆ Finally, neaten by covering the first line of stitching with a line of slightly larger, closer zigzag.

FABRICS WITH A PILE

For appliqué incorporating fabrics with a pile, for example velvets and corduroys, draw the design on the wrong side of the background fabric.

☆ Tack the top fabric and background together with right sides uppermost.

☆ Machine through with an open zigzag from the wrong side.

☆ Turn the work over. Trim away the surplus fabric cutting close to the stitching. Then cover the cut edge and first line of stitching with a close zigzag.

LEATHER, SUEDES AND PLASTICS

☆ Cut out the shape to be applied.

☆ Bond it onto the background fabric or hold it fast.

☆ Machine over the cut edges with an open zigzag. If the stitches are machined too closely together they will tend to split the leather or plastic. A line of splits will tend to develop into a cut along the inside edge of the stitching.

TRANSPARENT FABRICS

☆ For machine appliqué and cutwork techniques combining transparent or flimsy fabrics, draw the design onto paper.

☆ Tack the fabrics together with the paper on top.

☆ Tear the paper away when the stitching is complete.

FUR FABRICS

Fur fabrics should be cut and placed so that the fibres follow the fall of natural hair, usually to be stroked downwards.

☆ Draw the outline of the shape to be applied on the wrong side of the fabric.

☆ Cut out the shape, taking care to part not cut the fur with a pointed pair of scissors.

☆ Using a ballpoint needle, open zigzag and matching thread machine with the lie of the fur, keeping the fibres free of the stitching by holding them to one side.

☆ Finally, stroke or brush the fur to cover the stitching.

SUGGESTED READING
S. Gail Reeder. *Successful Machine Appliqué based on Techniques Developed by Barbara Lee.* Yours Truly, 1978.
Christine Risley. *Machine Embroidery – a complete guide.* Studio Vista, London, 1973.
Jennifer Gray. *Machine Embroidery: Technique and Design.* B.T. Batsford Ltd.
Moira McNeill. *Machine Embroidery: Lace and See Through Techniques.* B.T. Batsford, 1986.

PROJECT 12
FISH

This fish is all lines, angles, and curves.

You will need:
- *two different plain fabrics, approx. 25 × 25cm (10 × 10in)*
- *suitable threads*
- *swing needle sewing machine*
- *machine instruction manual*
- *small pair of sharp, pointed scissors*

1 Transfer a fish from design sheets 21, 22 and 23 onto the top fabric. Tack the two layers together around the outside edge of the pieces of fabric.

2 Thread up the machine. Set the stitch to zigzag.

3 Check the stitch tension is correct on a small test piece cut from the same fabric.

4 Place the fabric under the pressure foot. Lower the foot. With the needle in the fabric on the line begin stitching. It is easier to begin with a long straight line or gentle curve.

5 Cover all the lines with stitching, moving the machine carefully around the curves and angles.

6 When the stitching is complete cut away some parts of the top layer to expose the layer beneath.

EXTENSION IDEAS
You could place a transparent fabric over the machine piece and machine additional designs around the fish. When the stitching is complete cut away parts of the transparent layer.

Alternatively, put the fish piece into an embroidery ring and set the machine for free stitching, adding finer patterns and textures to the fish and the background.

9 THREE-DIMENSIONAL APPLIQUÉ

As we have seen, multi-layered appliqué techniques lend themselves to three-dimensional work. The contours of indented ridges, multi-layered stacks of colour or texture, and the soft edges achieved through layered and cutwork techniques correspond to layered structures in nature and carved surfaces of relief sculpture. The structure of shells, a cabbage cut straight through its centre, rock formations and fungi, all provide interesting starting points for three-dimensional work.

Folded squares and triangles, rectangles and circles applied in series can be built into faceted surfaces. These can have design links with architecture. Next time you drive into a city look at the structural grids and faceted surfaces of buildings with three-dimensional appliqué in mind.

Squares, triangles, rectangles and circles can be folded to form detached shapes and attached together to make a three-dimensional construction.

STUMPWORK

Areas of detached stitching, padded shapes and applied motifs give stumpwork or 'raised work' its three-dimensional quality. Stumpwork evolved from Elizabethan embroidery in which the plaited gold stems and petals or leaves worked in detached buttonhole stitch were raised from the background. The applied motifs, called 'slips', were worked on fine canvas or linen and then carefully cut out and applied onto silk.

113 *A bridegroom's head-dress from Rajasthan.*

This is made from hundreds of folded squares of brightly coloured cottons threaded between beads and little stuffed animals and birds hung from a wire frame.

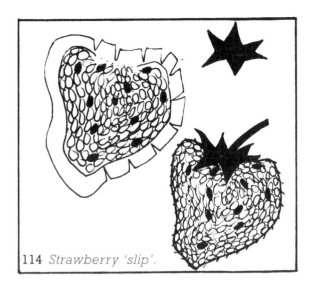

114 *Strawberry 'slip'.*

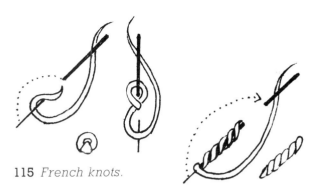

115 *French knots.*

116 *Bullion knots.*

There are several ways in which raised or softly padded forms can be achieved. Raised stitched textures can be worked on calico using closely packed embroidery stitches, perhaps french knots or bullion knots.

☆ Draw an outline of the shape onto calico and fill it with closely packed embroidery. When the stitching is complete cut it out, allowing for a border all around.

☆ Tuck this under, snipping to ease curves where necessary. Stitch the slip in position on a background fabric stretched in a ring or over a frame. Use tiny stitches in a matching thread.

117 *Canvas work panel, 30 × 18cm (12 × 7in), Lilian Harris, 1984.*

This canvas work panel combines a variety of stitches worked in wools and different embroidery threads. The sides of the houses have been folded down and stitched at the corners so that they stand out from the background. The roofs are applied leather. The whole piece is laced over a block of soft board.

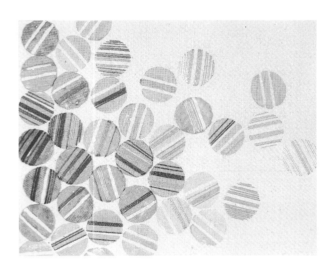

118 Circles, *15 × 20cm (5 × 7in) Vicky Lugg, 1983.* (The Embroiderers' Guild)

A circular block, perhaps a cork wrapped with string or a section of dowelling, with grooves cut in it, has been used to make a simple print on calico.

Separate prints have been cut out and applied over circles of card with long, straight stitches. Similar stitches have been added across some of the printed circles or used to make more circles on the areas of plain calico. These lines vary in colour, density and direction and set up a subtle sense of movement.

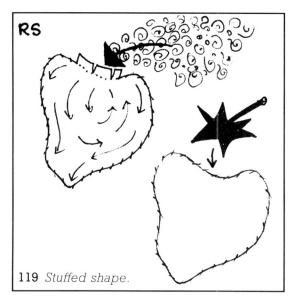

119 *Stuffed shape.*

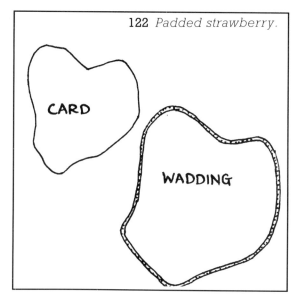

122 *Padded strawberry.*

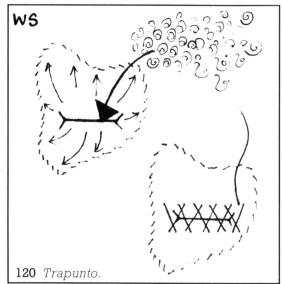

120 *Trapunto.*

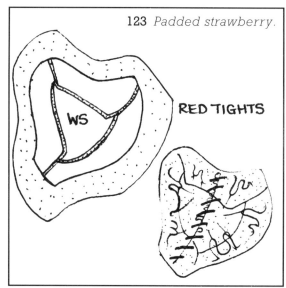

123 *Padded strawberry.*

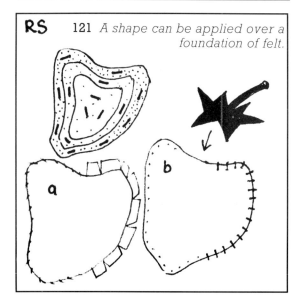

121 *A shape can be applied over a foundation of felt.*

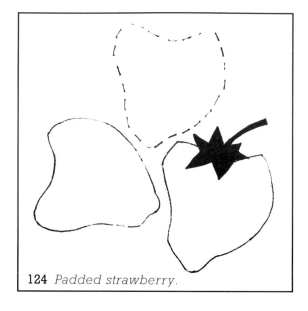

124 *Padded strawberry.*

A shape may be applied over a foundation of felt. This method is particularly suitable for non-woven fabrics, such as leathers, suedes, felt and plastic (fig. 121).

☆ Stretch the background fabric taut in a frame.

☆ Cut out the felt shape slightly smaller than the shape to be applied.

☆ Fasten this onto the background fabric with small stab stitches.

☆ Place the fabric shape over the felt shape. Sew the edges down well within the cut edges onto the background with hem stitch. To ensure that the stitches are even it can be helpful to mark out and make holes on the wrong side beforehand.

Some fabrics need turning under. Shapes for these should be cut larger and snipped to ease the corners and curves. Place the fabric shape over the felt shape. Tuck the turnings under the loose edges of the felt. Hem the turned edge down onto the background (fig. 121a).

Extra padding can be achieved with several felt shapes, each cut slightly smaller than the last and placed in a layered stack. The fabric shape is placed over this and the turnings, if any, are tucked under and sewn down with hem stitch. This gives a smooth softly rounded shape.

A card base or base of pelmet interfacing will give a crisp, rigid alternative to felt. Vicky Lugg's piece in the Embroiderers' Guild study folios demonstrates this very simply (fig. 118). Some of the velvet leaves in the window box of Constance Howard's *Silver Jubilee* hanging are crinkled while others are slightly stuffed (figs 90 and 91).

An applied shape can be stuffed by gently pushing loose Terylene wadding, kapok, wool, even shredded tights (pantyhose), through an unstitched section of the outline. To avoid bumps, push the stuffing in in very small amounts, first into all the corners with a fine knitting needle or stiletto. Then fill in the rest of the space. Beware – an overstuffed shape will tend to distort the surrounding fabric. When the stuffing is in place complete the stitching.

The space between the applied fabric and the background fabric can be stuffed after the stitching is completed with a form of *trapunto*.

☆ Complete the appliqué.

☆ Turn the work over to the wrong side.

☆ Make a small slit in the background fabric in the centre of the applied design.

☆ Then stuff the shape gently from the back, through the slit, using loose terylene wadding, wool, or kapok. First fill the corners and then fill the space evenly.

☆ Draw the slit closed with a line of herringbone or by over casting over the cut. Fasten off securely.

☆ Turn the work back to the right side (fig. 120).

Softly padded shapes can be made over thin card or pelmet interfacing and layers of wadding covered with stretched tights (pantyhose) (fig. 123).

Detached shapes can be made and neatened with the machine in various ways (Fig. 111), but partially applied with other techniques. The leaves on Sheila Gussin's embroidered panel are a good example of this (fig. 112).

STARTING POINTS

A park on a sunny afternoon is full of family groups framed between trees and flower beds. Rows of deck chairs, wooden benches, a bandstand, the swings and climbing frame all provide strong, simple design structures on which to place figures and explore stance and character.

A village cricket match – the simplicity of the white figures set in a great expanse of green; a knot of footballers; a crowded swimming pool; or a ballet lesson all provide a great variety of shapes within limited colour schemes.

The architecture of many railway stations provides a marvellous backdrop against which to set groups of travellers or isolated figures. Subtle tonal differences, the sombre atmosphere and divisions of space could be very simply explored, perhaps by a series of figure silhouettes cut from different suiting fabrics, tweeds and worsted samples, with areas of brighter wools and embroidery.

Queues anywhere are worth studying for mood and social comment. These suggestions are based on figures but lots of ideas for three-dimensional appliqué can be triggered by displays of fruit and vegetables. Imagine softly-padded oranges set in a basket of crushed green fabric.

You may think that ideas like these are exciting but difficult to express in fabric and thread. Many of the line drawings on the design sheets, particularly *Miss Piggy* on design sheet 24, could provide a starting point from which to try out and compare several different three-dimensional appliqué techniques. However, there are other simple ideas that can help:

☆ To start your own ideas look around you.

125 *Drawing of* The Sunbathers, *Pat Sales.*

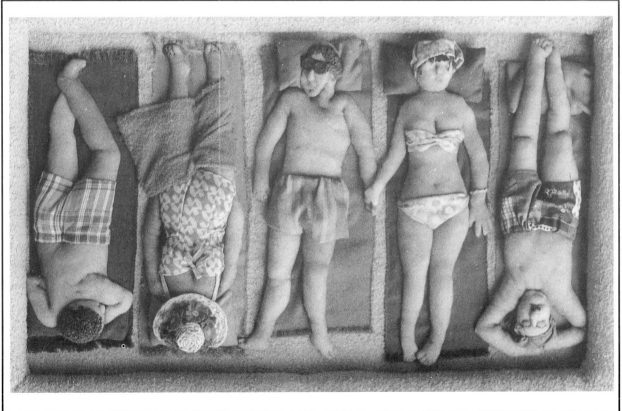

126 *Appliqué of* The Sunbathers, *Pat Sales.*

The Sunbathers *marked the beginning of Pat Sale's inventive work notable for its infectious sense of fun. She began this piece by drawing a row of people sunbathing on the beach, complete with silly hats and sunglasses. Simplifying the drawing, she traced their silhouettes and cut them out in card. She then covered the card with a layer of Terylene wadding. Next she stretched part of an old pair of tights (pantyhose) over the wadding and laced this securely on the back and trimmed the surplus tights (pantyhose) away. At this stage the bodies could be modelled by re-distributing the stuffing or adding a bit more in places – perhaps stitching on another stuffed piece, or stab stitching here and there. A line of running stitches pulled up into gathers gave them form and character. Then the fun began. Yellow french knots for a curly blonde, a knotted hankie and the straw hat, and so on.*

The Sunbathers *has been followed by* Beryl's Cookie, Bubbles, 'In The Best Possible Taste', Adam and Eve *and* The Three Graces. *In each panel, Pat has developed her ideas and working method a stage further. Later figures are sectioned up and cut into several strong shapes. Padded, wrapped, modelled and dressed, these are re-assembled in a carefully thought-out order and applied onto a background fabric stretched taut over a permanent frame. Each part is held in place by stitching from the back of the panel, through the tights (pantyhose) wrapped round at the back of the shapes and back through the background fabric, drawing them securely together. Any form of stitching*

around the edge would spoil the fleshy outlines.

Pat carefully selects just the right fabrics to express each character, mood and style from a special collection of bits and pieces. She loves rich combinations of colour and texture and collects fine old velvets, patterned silks, tiny beads and braids, scraps of fur, net and lace like a magpie. Finding exactly the right combination of colour, texture and pattern to work on a small scale is far from easy, but she achieves quite luscious effects. Her shapely ladies always ellicit laughter and an irresistible urge to prod.

☆ Think and look at groups of people or objects with appliqué in mind.

☆ A title may occur to you. List the characters or objects you would want to include. Decide on the mood or ideas you want to express.

☆ Go out with a camera to gather detailed information from every point of view. Make lots of drawings, however simple.

☆ Begin to gather and sort suitable fabrics and threads.

These ideas may tend to be muddled and rather too elaborate at first. Gradually try to sort them out and reduce your ideas to the barest essentials. Perhaps just one figure is enough to begin with.

☆ Look at your drawings and photographs carefully. Scan over them with a L-shaped view finder and search for: an interesting combination of characters or objects; simple design structures, i.e. strong background shapes or a constructional idea; a satisfying balance between dark and light areas; a lively mix of colour, pattern and texture; shapes which lend themselves readily to appliqué techniques; the interesting use of fabrics.

☆ Trace the main outlines from a photograph or make a linear drawing of just the mainshapes, no more. Scale this up to a workable size (fig. 97). Make two copies, one to be the master plan which, if necessary, could provide a 'map' for the background fabric on which to re-assemble the applied shapes. Cut up the other one to make patterns for the separate pieces.

127 In The Best Possible Taste, *Pat Sales.*

☆ Think through the order in which the design should be worked. The paper cut out shapes will help you do this. Plan and complete the work required on the background fabric before the three-dimensional shapes are applied. Stretch the background fabric taut over a permanent frame. Model the figures or objects, arrange them in position and stitch them into place. Add any finishing touches, perhaps quilting, embroidered details or if buttons, beads, laces, ribbons and other bits and bobs.

SUGGESTED READING
Muriel Best. *Stumpwork*. B.T. Batsford Ltd, 1987.
Hannah Frew Patterson. *Three Dimensional Embroidery*. UNR, 1975.

(Above and page 92)   **128** and **129** The Country Wife, *400 × 550cm (157 × 216in), Constance Howard.* (Northampton Museum and Art Gallery)

In 1950 Constance Howard was asked by F.H.K. Henrion to make a large embroidered panel for the Festival of Britain. She enlisted the help of her students, and The Country Wife *was exhibited the following year. It now hangs in Denman College, the headquarters of the Women's Institute in Oxford.*

It is a very large piece, hung unframed, and worked on five widths of open weave furnishing fabric, joined by flat overlapped seams stitched onto a backing fabric with herringbone stitch.

The composition is organized like a stage set with a backdrop of scenes from village life. The main shapes of the church, homes and gardens, farms and orchards are applied in wools, and the details embroidered very directly. Notice the vegetable plot, the hens, and the clouds scudding across the sky. In front of these, women and children shop at an open marquee or hat-stall. A doe-eyed choir on one side is balanced by a solitary man rehearsing a flock of

ladies on the other. Opened up and centre stage, the church hall is filled with women busily preoccupied with every kind of craftwork. Their children are helping. Toys and family pets are included.

In all there are thirty-nine women, one man, seven children and six animals! The panel is imbued with a sense of well ordered cooperative female industry, and illustrates the role of women in the 1950s. The colour and feel of the applied wools, the checks and tweeds, are an example of the way in which the fabrics reflect the times in which a piece is made.

Some of the craftwork was specially made by members of the Women's Institute. The real pair of scissors and a tape measure amongst the cleverly modelled and applied inventions give an idea of the scale of the piece and the key to its popular appeal.

Looked at closely, this hanging contains so many of the appliqué techniques explored in this book that it is worth lingering over the details a moment longer to recognize and enjoy them again.

129 *Detail of* The Country Wife, *Constance Howard*

SUPPLIERS

UNITED KINGDOM
Mail order service available

Borovick Fabrics Ltd
16 Berwick Street
London W1V 4HP
(Organzas, shot silk, satins and nets, etc.)

Felt and Hessian Shop
34 Grencille Street
London EC1
(Felt and hessians)

Iqbal Textiles
394–396 Stapleton Road
Bristol
(Shot organzas, chiffons, satins, silks, etc.)

John Lewis
Oxford Street
London W1
Other local branches too
(Wools, cottons, polyesters and furnishing fabrics, etc.; quilting, waddings and lining fabrics; very good range of tools and haberdashery)

Liberty & Co. Ltd
Regent Street
London
W1
(Exotic and high quality fabrics; Liberty lawns)

*Livingstone Textile Co. Ltd
St Michael's Lane
Bridport
Dorset
(Cottons and patterned fabrics; calico, dyed cotton drill, polyester, etc. in large quantities)

*Maculloch and Wallis
25–26 Derwig Street
London W1R 0BH
(Traditional basic embroidery fabrics)

*Mace and Nairn
89 Crane Street
Salisbury
Wiltshire
(Good range of traditional embroidery fabrics)

*The Patchwork Dog and Calico Cat
21 Chalk Farm Road
London NW1
(Plain and patterned pure cottons)

*60 Plus Textiles
Barley
Nelson
Lancs
(Patchwork bales, shiring and sheeting)

*Strawbery Fayre
Chagford
Newton Abbot
Devon TQ13 8EN
(Plain and patterned pure cottons)

*Whalleys (Bradford) Ltd
Harris Court
Great Horton
Bradford
(Wide range of natural and specialist fabrics; silks, cottons, wools, etc.)

AMERICA

Alice Peterson's Needlworks
11733 Barrington Court
Los Angeles, Ca.

Cabin Fever Calicoes
Box 6256
Washington, D.C.
20015

The Friday Needlework Shop
1260 Delaware Ave,
Buffalo, N.Y.

Gutcheon Patchworks
Dept 8
611 Broadway
New York
N.Y. 10012

Jeweled Needle
920 Nicollet Mall
Minneapolis, Minn.

The Knittery
2040 Union Street
San Francisco, Ca.

Lazy Daisy
602 E. Walnut Street
Pasadena, Ca.

Lucy Cooper Hill
9570 Bay Harbor Terrace
Miami Beach, Florida

Needlecraft Shop
13561 Ventura Blvd
Sherman Oaks, Ca.

Needlework
Whaler's Wharf, Building 10-A Berth 76
San Pedro, Ca.

Nimble Needle
2645 San Diego Ave
San Diego, Ca.

The Spinning Wheel
1612 J. Street
Modesto, Ca.

The Stearns & Foster Co.
Cincinnati, Ohio 45215
(For quilting needles)

Yarn Depot
545 Suttee Street
San Francisco, Ca.

Yarn Tree
101-L West 5th Ave
Scottsdale, Arizona

Yarncrafters Ltd
3146 M Street N.W.
Georgetown, Washington, D.C.

Index

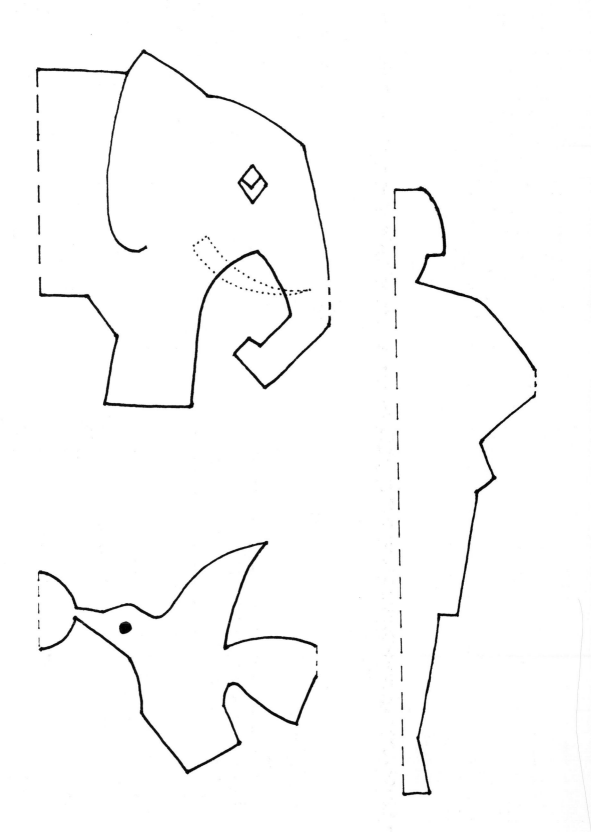

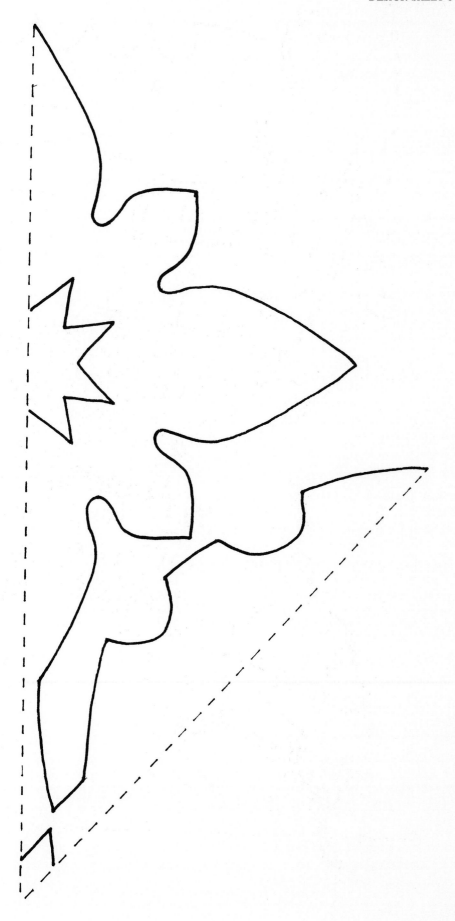

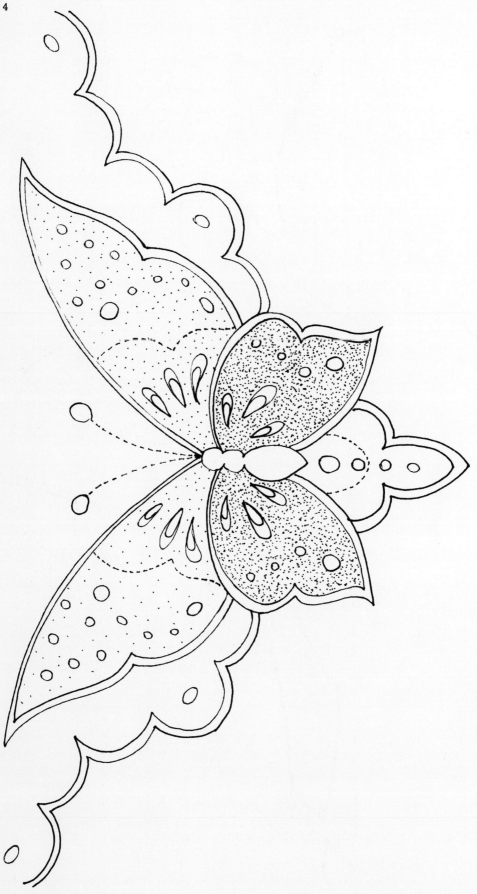

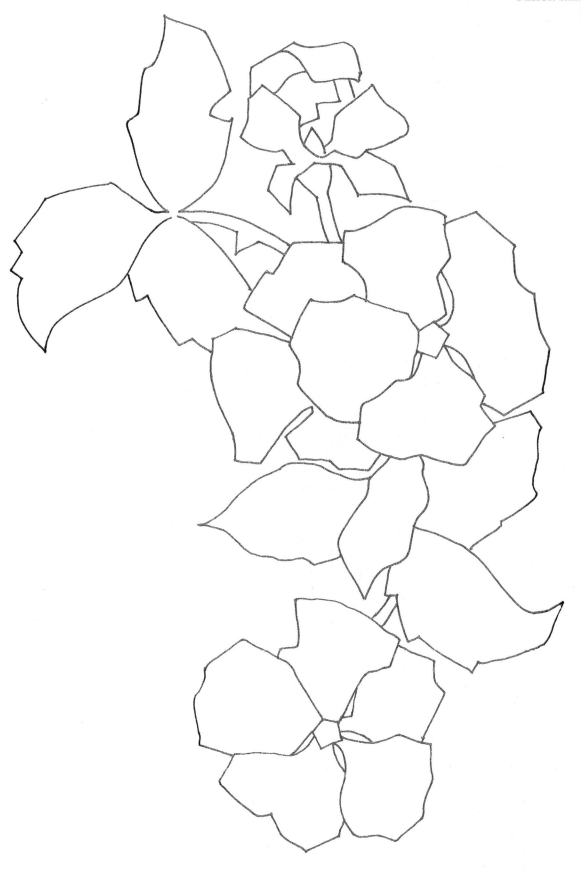

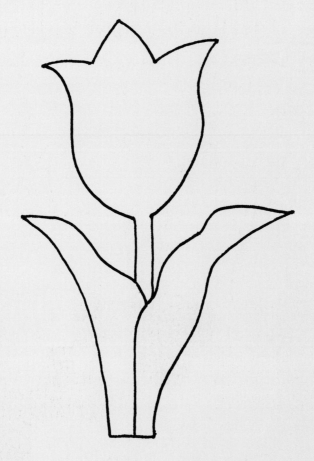

85cm

8·5cm

8.5cm (3¼in)

8·5cm (3¼in)

2.5cm(1in)

2·5cm(1in)

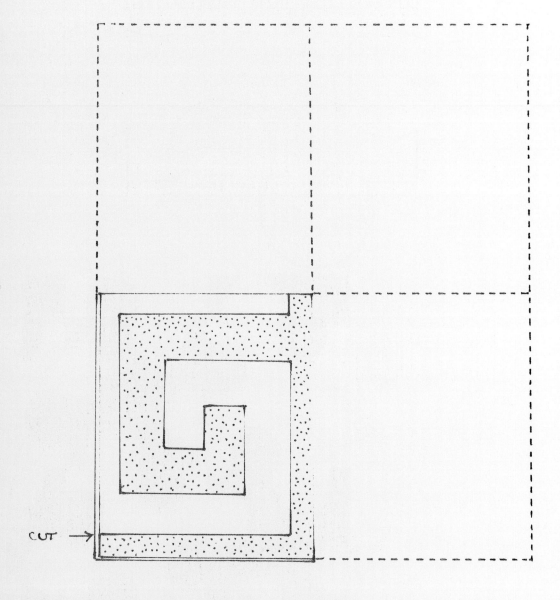

CUT →

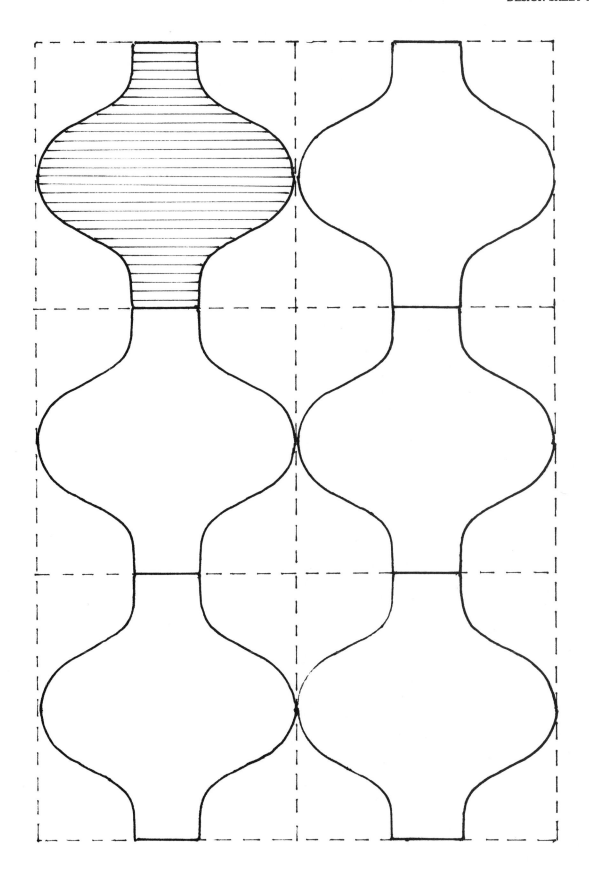

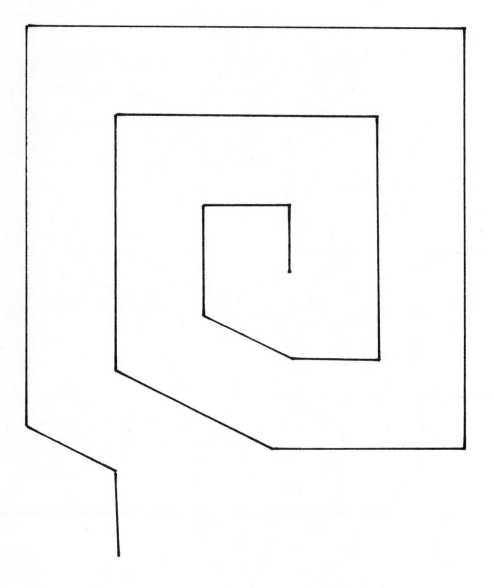

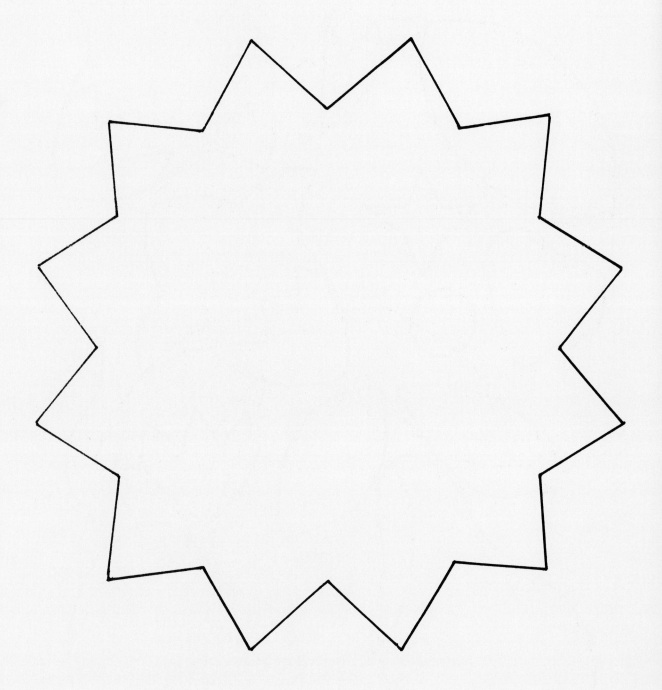

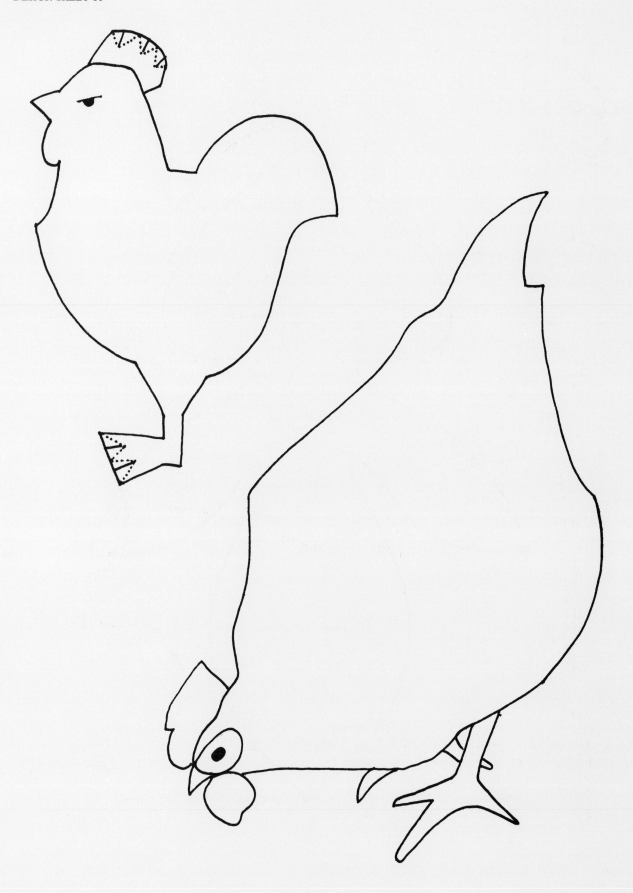

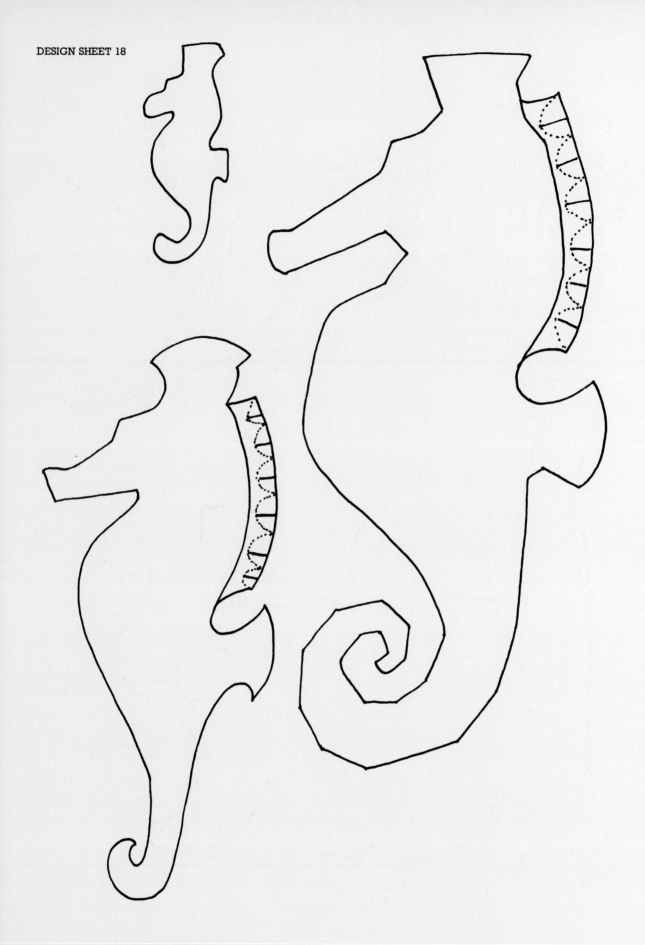

START

FINISH

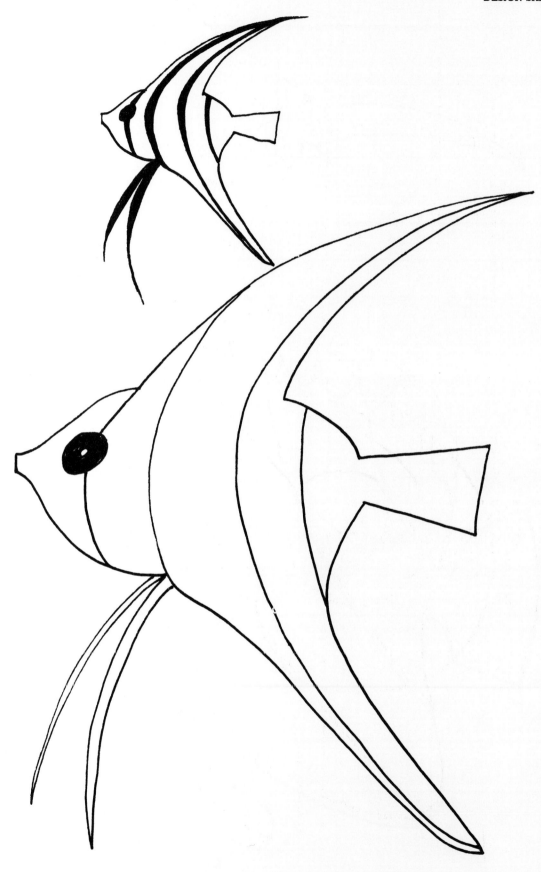

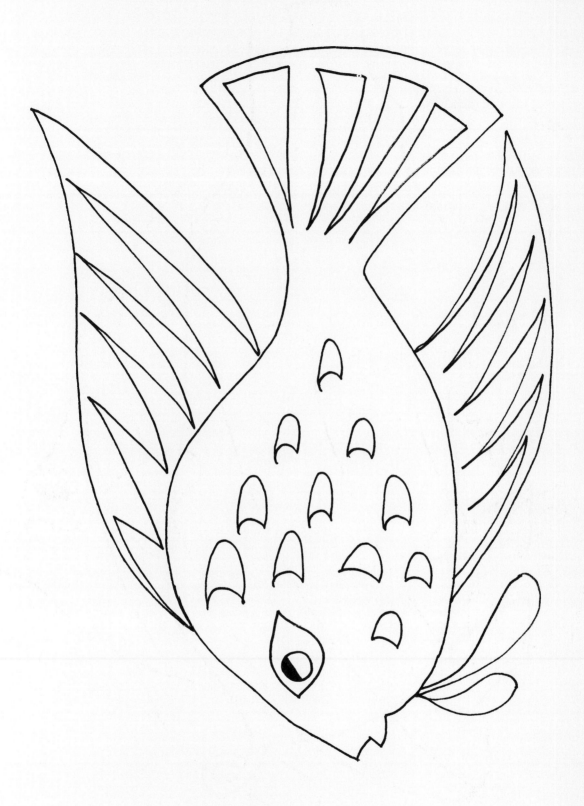